# The Message Game

Written by Ice White

Olcan Print
Part of the Olcan Group
London
www.olcan.co

First published by Olcan Press on 7rd January 2020
Olcan Print/Press are a subsidiary of the Olcan Group
6 Park Hill, Ealing
London, W5 2JN, UK
Email: team@olcan.co
www.olcan.co

For permission contact:
team@olcan.co

A CIP record of this publication is available from the British Library.
First printed June 2019

Paperback
ISBN: 978-1-9160006-5-0

# THE MESSAGE GAME

## A GUIDE TO HAVING THE POWER OF DATING AT THE TOUCH OF A BUTTON

### A TINDER AND ONLINE DATING GUIDE FOR MEN

# WRITTEN BY ICE WHITE

*This is dedicated to every man out there that wants to improve everything about himself.*

# Chapters

# General Disclaimers & Information

This book contains screenshots of conversations. For the privacy, safety and security of those involved, names, photos, phone numbers and other forms of easily identifiable personal information have been removed or covered. Some screenshots have little images of Ice's face to cover up such information, other screenshots may have other edits including scribbles. However, everything has been described as comprehensively and as simple as possible, and all identities have been censored.

It will highly benefit you to join the Facebook group and the Telegram group to see updates. Also follow mee on social media so you can see the world this all happens in.

**Facebook Group:**
Ice White's Message  Game
Facebook.com/groups/MessageGame

**Telegram Group:**
Message Game
(See Facebook Group)

**Websites:**
GameGlobal.net

**Instagram:**
IceWhiteOfficial

**Facebook:**
Ice White

Ain't gonna lie Ice Spontaneous line
still has pulling power in 2018!! 18:11

Hey dude, just wanted to say how
fucking sick your message game piece
is. Out of the first five matches I had. I
got 3 of their numbers straightaway
within about four text messages. It's
solid, but I toned it down a bit as I was
speaking with older women. Fucking
cheers geez! Thanks for posting

I reduced my tinder usage time by 80%

12:46

thanks for the huge value
you provided in your tinder
document. Have you
thought about providing a
service where you go
through a person's text
game and decipher,
annotate and provide
solutions. I know that would
help a lot of guys out there.

Further demonstration why you
absolutely rock at message game

21:50

Hey mate! saw your message game file
you uploaded. it's insanely interesting
and teaching a lot. so thanks for that!
I'd like to ask, what apps are being used
in this entire file? i could only recognize
whatsapp and tinder. Thanks ☺

⊢̶ ̶ ̶ ̶ ̶ ̶ ̶ ̶ ̶: Some girl shouted you out on
her insta, that you where the best at texting
girls. How do you do it? Just lots of practice?

Overall I thought it was fun to read and
pretty informative. Thanks for sharing
🤜

17:41

# This improved my test game 10x

yeah, off topic i wanna say i'm very
thankful this chat exists and i wanna
thank everyone in here for providing
value, good shit

14:43

👍 cant wait to see the finished book.
Keep up the good work! You a pro

13:41

holy shit, I'd give you a bj for this if i
was homo, thanks for sharing!

13:09

@IceWhiteOfficial I just read your message game. You are a god I was wasting my time for years 14:12

Who else said let me just have a look and ended up reading the whole thing? 13:43

You're free thing helped me and a bro out so much that he used lets skip the bullshit how spontaneous are you and pulled off tender the first night.

Bro you saved my tinder game. Never experienced getting girls so fast in my home 16:22

Dude, literally just read your message game guide like 5 hours ago decided to put into practice on a girl that already wanted to fuck me, but the escalation now is fucking insane dude!! And I just reply less and less and she keeps coming, life saver bro thank you!!

This was... No words honestly. Seen nothing else quite like it. 09:27

hey bro you're great..read your tinder material..your super funny and witty and it gave me great results..thank you soo much..your awesome

Dude that PDF you sent me...I finished it within an hour. None of the RSD coaches is as efficient as you are. 4 years and a half in game and this blew my mind. It may seem selfish to ask you for more, but how do you become that good? Practice can't be the one and only secret. Cheers

This is a really cool guide. Practical and informative. Thanks alot mate 08:59

Big fan of your tinder manual, btw 20:28

Your system does work man. I just started using it. I have gotten so fast numbers. I pulled and closed her on Tuesday at my place. Could be strong fuck buddy in future so I hide the details 19:33

# Intro

When I was 14, there was a girl who walked on the same street at around the same time each day on the way to school. We went to different high schools, so I would head south and she would head north, but on that very street, we both had to go east. We didn't really know each other, but we were connected on Facebook. She was 15. We were both interested in each other but never really went out of our own way to meet face to face; perhaps it was the naivety of being teens as well as being too physically shy. But we would message each other, quite a lot. This is when I really first wondered about the possibilities of making things happen by messaging. I was just a young man in need of a high school sweetheart. I wanted to talk to her. I wanted to kiss her. I wanted to be with her. By exchanging messages, I eventually came to imagine a question or a possibility that goes even deeper; is messaging just a maze of possibilities that I could eventually figure out in order to make this happen? Is there a way to talk to her, kiss her and be with her?

I cannot be the only one asking these questions.

Many girlfriends and failed relationships later, I finally figured it out, and after feedback from hundreds of people who loved a simple guide I created about messaging, it is time for a book. Lives have been changed. Possibilities have been shown. Following my mid-teen years came many dating opportunities and adventures that are hugely owed to how I have communicated effectively in order to take girls out that I am interested in. I cannot change the past, but I can create the future.

Fast-forward a few years and I have dated models, even though when I was younger I did not speak much. I went from being quiet to being fortunate enough to date a model.

I have had dates every single day in the space of two weeks, but when I was younger, I was addicted to playing computer games. I went from a virtual world to having amazing but real experiences.

I have had sex with multiple girls in the space of a few hours, but I used to be lonely. I went from zero to hero.

I have many awesome stories to tell you, but it was never always like this before. Now that these skills have been figured out and acquired, these skills are for life. I will never face the same dating problems ever again, and here I will show you many things to help you get there.

My name is Ice, and I am a computer game addict that transformed into a computer game creator and a dating coach. It's a little like saying you're a comic book nerd and that you also have a girlfriend. But jokes aside, there is absolutely nothing to say that you cannot achieve what you are about to see in this book. If you make excuses or think you cannot do this, you are lying to yourself. If you want to go through life making excuses and not becoming the best you want to be, put this fucking book down and give it to someone who will use it to help themselves.

So who am I? Why should you give a fuck?

I believe that dating, and the communication that goes with it, has become far too complicated. I have been there. I have struggled. I have been lost. I have been through lots of relationships that did not last. I have been blocked.

But I have also got through. I have succeeded. I have found the way. I have made lots of relationships happen, even if they did not last.

Over the course of 10 years, I have worked out various things, and eventually I found the big picture. This is easier than you think. I have dated many women with the help of the mindset and techniques I developed myself. I have found myself girlfriends, dates and sexual relationships, and you will be able to replicate that.

When someone says the word *'dating'*, people flinch, people get scared, people get nervous; people get skeptical or feel sick or anxious. Even more so, people get depressed by the very idea that in order to find someone suitable, you will probably have to wait a very long time. You would probably have to face rejection from those who you thought were good for you, and you would probably end up in some kind of a relationship only for it to be over before you know it. Dating is not easy, but I am here to help simplify it for you.

But let me emphasize something. This is not a book for you to find 'the one'. This is not your happy ending yet. This is a book to maximize your chances at dating. No more boring dates or **bullshit** messaging that goes nowhere. Let's make dating fun, and let's make messaging as useful and beneficial as possible. Whether you want to meet many girls or find one special person, this is for you. If you're not ready to change, you're not ready to live.

I want you to view *'message game'* as a puzzle, but you don't have the box so you don't know what the full picture is. All you have are all these random pieces and you don't know what to do other than to blindly try. With that in mind, each chapter will give you a piece of that puzzle for you to fit together. Eventually you will see the full picture more clearly. These puzzle pieces will include the likes of Tinder, WhatsApp, Facebook, Instagram, Snapchat and more. By the end of putting the puzzle together, you would have acquired the information and mindset you need to maximize your dating chances on these messaging platforms. Again, whether that's to get yourself 100 dates or to get yourself a wife, this will help you.

At the end of most chapters, there are screenshots of my own messages that I have collected over time. These are not just screenshots of messages, these are ways to show you how fast and effective a minimal amount of messages can maximize what you actually want. Things like getting phone numbers from Tinder in two messages, things like getting a date in 'just a few' messages, and the context and stories behind the messages. My own personal messages will be shown on the left side of certain pages.

Most guys have a particular crush, or perhaps a lot of specific f females that they are interested in. But from the thousands of guys I have met and thousands of messages I have been requested to look at and criticize, it is clear that most guys do not know what they are doing; or do not know how to actually get what they want. I have helped guys get Valentine's Day dates in one message. That is nothing compared to the hundreds of personal experiences you are about to see.

Some chapters will also include other people's messages; messages from followers who requested as to where they went wrong. So not only will you see the good side, you will also see the bad side so you can learn what you should avoid doing yourself. Things like desperation, neediness, wasting time, not getting to the point, etc. Messages from other people will be shown on the right side of certain pages.

Finally, you will be given assignments. This means you will be given exact instructions to test out some little skills you need to pick up on the way.

Now, are you ready for some real **pimpspiration** ?

**Tinder**

This is called the **spontaneous line.** I first used it in 2017.

The opener calls for involvement. It is interactive and therefore much more response provoking and action stimulating.

'Let's *skip all the **bullshit**'* implies that there is no time to waste, and it calls for a skipping of the bullshit formalities that everyone else does. We are not here to discuss our life stories… we are here to meet.

'*How spontaneous are you?* 'Calls for her involvement. It is interactive and puts the power on you because you are throwing a test at her.

After her response, you have the information you need. You have **screened** her. Now get her number so you can get organized. This is called **number-closing.**

# Getting Started: What Is The First Thing You Need To Do?

In some chapters, I will ask you a question in the beginning. You must ask yourself the same question, but in first person. So ask yourself.

*'What is the first thing I need to do?'*

Tips before you begin.
1. Do not ever skip ahead; you will miss out on amazing things.
2. Forget everything you thought you knew about m messaging girls.

Needless to say, back in the days we did not have screens. Hundreds of years ago people met and if they wanted to meet again, they would go to a regular place or a location where one party lives. Sure, you also had carrier pigeons and letters, but most people centuries ago could not read or write. However, once telephones became a thing, it became a little easier.

Now imagine it is 1986. I f you meet someone in a nightclub, at a beach or anywhere else, the only way of communicating in order to meet a gain was by phone. One person would have to use a payphone or a phone at home or work to call the other person, but the catch is that the person being called must be at the geographical location of that phone which is being called.

Let us fast-forward to the year 2010. People have phones in their pockets. There is now a new thing called 'messages' where people can press buttons to write words to send to other people's phones which are in their pockets. Radical! Now that it's not 2010 anymore, we have various forms of extra communication like Facebook, Instagram, Snapchat, LinkedIn and much more all at the same time. See, now it is complicated. We have more access, but that does not mean it is easier.

What you need to see most importantly about this situation is that there are now more barriers between you and who you want to meet, even though it may appear as if there are so many more ways to find someone or communicate with someone. In 1986, if someone said they will be "there", they WILL be there. In 2019, if someone says they will be there, they could change their mind spontaneously and let you know without a hindrance of guilt by sending you a message at any time that they will NOT be there for whatever reason. That's the power of time.

In this age, everyone uses social media to project a better version of themselves. Social media as used by most people, in most cases, is fake. The online world is all fake. Photos are faked every single minute with filters and edits. Photos are often prepared for, arranged or posed for. So much you see is fake. Drop your expectations when you see something utterly amazing, because whatever photo you see of a girl on Tinder, Facebook or Instagram is probably the pinnacle of all recorded experiences in her lifetime according to a still image that she has access to. When most people design their profiles, they do so in a very positive way in order to put across a good projection of themselves. In 1986, none of this existed. Life was seemingly more simple. You see a girl and that's it. No messaging. No looking at photos. And on her side, she is not taking so m any photos for the purpose of validation of drawing attention to herself online. 1986 is humble. 2015 onwards is staged, attention-seeking and complicated. We did not want this, but we can solve it for you. Anyone else is just stuck.

The technology we have today makes it easier to find people now that we have instant access to billions of people through searches. However, the equally negative version of it all is that anyone, at any moment, can cancel on you, block you or influence in an unhealthy way how you see them or how they see you without even physically meeting. Now take that into consideration and remember one thing; if you want to have any kind of relationship with someone or meet someone, there's only one thing you should be aiming for - **meeting**. What else do you possibly need? This is no guide to satisfy your constant need for attention online; this is a guide to make things happen in the real world.

You can lay on your front on your bed with your legs up as if you're a teenage girl while giggling at 'funny messages', but that's not really the relationship you want in itself. You need to meet people. You need physical interaction. Your end goal is not to be giggling at a screen when you're in a room all alone, your end goal is to track this person down and have a meaningful connection in a realm of physical existence, not touching a screen to stimulate your brain or eradicate your boredom.

A common mistake is to think that it is better to *'get to know each other'* by exchanging words on a screen. It is not. Whether you have briefly met someone or never met someone but are able to message them, it is better to *'get to know each other'* by actually physically meeting. This is one of the most important things emphasized in this guide. If you have nothing but words on a screen, it is all meaningless. If you disagree, you are probably thinking about that time you had 'lots of fun' sending messages to someone. That is everything that ever happened, right? Now you get it. To take things further than just an interaction online, you need to focus on taking it offline into the physical world. Nobody cares about a conversation you had on Facebook. The story you could tell about a real adventure between you and the person you want to meet will **always** be far superior to any experience that was less than actually meeting. It's funny because SMS means *"Short Message Service"*; it's just a shame that people are not using it that way anymore.

The first thing you need to do is to get comfortable with the idea of taking full responsibility. No more blaming people or making excuses for the bad results you get when you send a message to a girl and don't get the response you wanted. It is time for you to make some changes and get better results, whether that is with Tinder or any other messaging platform. On top of that, you also need to think about the most basic and foundational things when you are messaging someone. You do not want to be that creepy guy without a profile picture. You also do not want to be the guy who needs to explain things. You need to be clear, and it also needs to be clear that you are not just some moron on the Internet that is a potential danger. You are a person. You exist. You have something to offer.

You need to realize that things are not going to happen randomly or magically for you. You need to make things happen. In the next chapters, you will find out how to make certain things happen by focusing on various aspects of messaging girls in order to get them to go out with you. Girls will not suddenly fall into your lap if you do absolutely nothing, you need to make some changes to what you have been doing so far. That's what this book is for. You have been lost all this time, but now it is time for you to be in control.

What I learned is that if something works for one person, it is likely to work on more people. If you find an ant, there is most likely a presence of more ants nearby; the ant must have come from somewhere. Where you find one of something, you will most likely find more of it. People. Oil. Trees. Birds. Fish. I f you can sell something to one person, you are able to sell it to another person. If you can get one girlfriend, you have no excuse of not being able to get another.

This book contains many WhatsApp conversations and many screenshots show myself or others asking for WhatsApp. WhatsApp is more common in some countries or cities than others, especially in cities like London where there is a massively dominant foreign population, which also brings in a large population of foreign phone numbers. WhatsApp makes it easy to message people with different country codes. It is advised that you research your city or country in terms of what the most popular messenger apps are; most countries use either Facebook messaging or WhatsApp primarily. This is discussed more in a lot of detail in the chapter **Platforms & Social Media.**

Do you wanna check out a churros place on Wednesday?

Euh yes 😊

SUN AT 19:06

It recently opened and it's a pretty cool place. I'm a big foodie.

Ok 😊

MON AT 22:28

What time you wanna meet? And anything else you wanted to do?

TUE AT 07:47

I don't know I just need to be at Victoria Coach Station at 10 am Thursday.

So when and you want 😊

TUE AT 09:00

*where

## Facebook

There's a backstory to this. I met this girl one time a year before this message was sent. Let's call her *Frenchie*. I met her in a club and that very night I started dating the friend she was with... let's call her friend *Tokyo*. A year later, I invited *Fenchie* and two other girls to my house; let's call the other two girls *Blondie* and *Latina*. All three came. *Blondie* left after a while because she had to be somewhere early in the morning, so I was left with *Frenchie* and *Latina*. I kicked *Frenchie* out into the rain and slept with *Latina*. Poor *Frenchie*.

A few days later, I took *Frenchie* out, despite kicking her out of the house a few days earlier to sleep with someone else. I took *Frenchie* out for some churros, as shown on the left, and I slept with her too.

All I did was ask a simple question, directly aiming at doing some kind of activity with her participation. Looks easy, right?

Also, notice that I managed to gain some extra information, so I know more things about what we will be doing. This is for Wednesday, but she mentioned Thursday morning; this implies her availability until a certain point. That certain point was the next day, and that implies she wants me to know she is available to fuck. And so... she did stay with me until that next day.

**19:12**

Stop blocking me on here, can you not come to me please? I am coming next Sunday. My parents kind of want to have dinner with you soon.

Sent from web

added you on Messenger

DECLINE          ACCEPT

**Facebook**

This girl made a new account just to message me.

This is just to prove that the power of this book can teach you things to the point where you can have girls chasing you even if you block them.

---

Saturday 22:44

Let's skip all the bullshit. How adventurous are you?

Depends on the day 😅 but trying to live a life and not just float and you?

Saturday 23:11

Well I am having some intense days and need some relaxation. But yes. Can you name 3 things you wanna do on our first date? ; )

Work has been intense?
Our? 😆 haha hm maybe eat laugh get to know you 🙈 and sing if we ended up at karaoke 😊

You have any things you wanna do?

Saturday 23:43

Yes. I'm a foodie, I hope you are. In which case, drop in your WhatsApp and let the feast begin. ; )

Of course i am 😊 ahah okay,
+42 **ICE ICE**

**Tinder**

For every message, a step is made in order to take it somewhere. This is the **adventurous line**. This opener calls for her cooperation and screens her so that I can see if she is fun or not. If she is fun, then our time together will be very straightforward.

There is then my response to her response, tied in with another follow up question centered around taking her out. This is the **3 things line**. It tells me what she wants to do, and then it would be extremely easy to take her on a date that she actually wanted. It makes things a lot more personal and fun for her.

Third, there is the move to WhatsApp.

Every single part here is centered on being progressive and taking her out.

# Knowing Your Goals: What Do You Want?

Ask yourself. *'What do I want?'*

Talk to her like you want her, but not like you need her. There is a difference. If you show neediness to a girl, she will know straight away that you need her. This is not attractive.

Teaching these methods over time, a common question put across was *'what would be the best response?'* First of all, it does not work like that. You cannot get a *'perfect response'*. People are different and respond to different things. There are over a million words in the English language, and that means there are literally trillions of ways that you could possibly lead a conversation and trillions more ways that you could respond with. Infinite ape theory is a theory that suggests that under the circumstances of monkeys hitting, at random, letters on a typewriter over an infinite amount of time, monkeys will almost surely, yet eventually, produce any of the entire works of Shakespeare, or potentially the lyrics to your favorite songs. Despite this fact, it will actually take the monkeys longer than the age of the Universe itself for them finally to write Shakespeare's work. That is just a philosophical theory to put into perspective how pointless it is for you to spend too much time thinking about what the perfect thing to say is. There is no perfect thing. The real question is *'what does this achieve?'* but that is still not enough.

Be careful what your question is. If you ask the wrong question, you will not get the answer you should be looking for.

What you really want is the independence to be able to do this for yourself. I am teaching you how to fish, and you must therefore be prepared to take control of your own destiny. Make your own conversations, the examples you see are just examples. Many people have copied and gained success, but you also need to be original in the sense that you should already know who you are and work out ways in which your communication matches that. I personally want to get things done; therefore, I believe in efficiency, therefore I should communicate efficiently. You may want to have fun conversations, therefore you must be fun, and therefore you must communicate in fun ways. It is important for you to be decisive and to take action. A girl will not do all the work for you; you can hardly ever rely on most girls to choose a restaurant. Girls like having a man who is capable enough to make the decisions.

I take it that you're not here to learn all this just to bake some cookies with some girl you like. Let's not pretend you're here for something other than sex. You may be using this to get this one particular girl out with you, or you may be using this to get lots of different dates so you can live a kind of life where you have the choice of lots of different girls. No judgement. But whatever you use this for, you need to know exactly what you want.

Do you want to have an awesome sex life? Alternatively, do you want to stay the same as you are now and not improve anything? Do you want to have a fun relationship with someone and do many fun things? Do you want to have dates with lots of girls or have sex with multiple girls within a short period? Do you want to date models? Do you want a really cute relationship? You need to understand your goals so you know what you have to do. This is all about communication. If you cannot communicate well, you will be less likely to make things happen because in order to make things happen, you need to either do everything yourself or have the help of others. You cannot do everything yourself every single time.

In the aspect of knowing what you want, you have to, at the very least, know what you want in the short term. Short term, you may want to meet a girl to see where it goes without thinking about the distant future, but if you are not showing her what you want, she will be asking herself what you want from her. In most cases, girls just see that guys are just wasting their time or that they just want sex.

Of course, there are plenty of places to meet people, but let's use Tinder as an example of one of them. Why use Tinder? To get matches. Why get matches? To get dates. The process is pretty simple, but most people don't match that with their thought process. Your thought process needs to be simplified. You are there to match with girls so you can take them out. All you have to do is match, talk, meet. That is a grand total of 3 simple things that you need to do. Once you have a match, all it takes is to communicate in order to complete the third step. Not all matches on Tinder talk. Not all talkers on Tinder meet. But every single time you meet someone from Tinder, it is far better than only getting to one of the first two steps.

What does this achieve? Well, here are a few things that achieve absolutely nothing:

1. Hello
2. Hi
3. Hey
4. How are you?

These are some of the useless messages you could ever send, the last one being the most useless three words in the history of communication. The person asking doesn't really care or want to know, and the person answering never responds truthfully to the question. Do you want a conversation like that? Would she? What often follows this opener or question is just a tragic meaningless exchange of basic words with absolutely no connection or meaning. Harvard researchers found that there are three things you can put into words that can build up a conversation:

1. Authenticity
2. Connection
3. Topic giving a taste of who you are

**Never** use *'how are you?'* Ever. There are better things to say, such as 'what are you looking forward to this month?' or 'what kind of food are you craving right now?' These two questions alone are of far better use in dating communication. The first question can have her reveal something she may be passionate about and something that she is obviously interested in and looking forward to, the second question brings to mind a sense of taste combined with some in-the-moment reality. You're reading this right now, what are you craving? Probably pizza, maybe ice cream, perhaps you haven't had cheesy fries for a while, or a very satisfying breakfast with waffles and orange juice.

What does she want? To summarize so far, she does not want a man who cannot make his mind up and cannot make decisions. She does not want a boring conversation. She does not want to open a message and see *'hi'* or *'how are you?'* If you send a message to someone saying just *'hi'* it is as if you are waiting for their permission to proceed with saying what you wanted to say. If you had to send an email to a CEO, you would have to be an idiot to just say *'hi'*, so why would you do the same to a girl? Conversations must have a sense of purpose.

Interestingly enough, I have been requested to write about 'dick pics' and 'nudes'. In simple terms, what would Jesus do? Just don't. Don't ever send a picture of your penis to someone. It's not nice. It's weird. Some people have had success with it, but seriously, what's the point? If she wants to see it, she can come to you and take a peek herself and maybe give it a stroke. There are some girls who are getting pictures of dicks left, right and center and they didn't even ask for any of it. It's not really something you should be doing, and there are far too many reasons for me to explain. One of those many reasons is something you would not expect. In conversation with a female friend, she told me that she had not had sex for 8 months, but that there was some guy she was interested in. She said she doesn't really want to see him because she is afraid that his dick is too big. This may not appear to be entirely logical, but that's exactly why the whole topic of d ick pics is ridiculous. I have never sent one and I never will. I'm sure she would be really fascinated by the shaft, the coloring and the pointiness, but it's a little like showing her a picture of your balls or your asscrack. It's not pictures of dicks that will make her like you, just like it will n ever be pictures of your balls. Ultimately, if you want to work your way into a girl's vagina, don't do it by scanning your asscheeks on a printer.

That leaves us with the topic of nudes. If you're a guy and you are sending nudes, I think you should reconsider what you are doing with your life. On the other hand, this topic is almost always about guys wanting to know how to get girls to send pictures of themselves naked or any other dirty pictures of them. I first received such images at the age of around 14 or 15, and that is fucking awesome when you're a kid. But when you are sent hundreds of them over time, it gets pretty boring and eventually you realize it's pretty pointless. Hard enough to believe myself, I never really asked for nudes, but I received plenty of them. Are you asking for nudes? Are you receiving them? Are you collecting them? Are you looking at them everyday? If the answer is yes, then you definitely lack physical sexual activity. The diagnosis is therefore that, at the end of the day, an arousing picture doesn't mean anything to what your body actually needs. You are not here to learn how to collect naked pictures of girls for your own validation and ego boost, you are here to learn how to maximize your communication opportunities with girls in order to maximize the satisfaction of your sex life and dating life, which will impact positively on your life overall.

In conclusion, you just need to simplify. This is the concept you should think about in order to understand what you actually need. You do not need photos of girls with their tits out or posing by a mirror showing some ass, you need girls to physically meet you and interact with you. You do not need to send pictures of dicks, you need to establish a connection and meet her so she can actually touch y our penis consensually. You need to know what you want and think about what she wants. You must also understand what she doesn't want. Don't make things complicated.

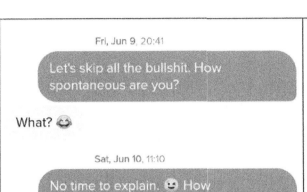

Fri, Jun 9, 20:41

Let's skip all the bullshit. How spontaneous are you?

What? 😅

Sat, Jun 10, 11:10

No time to explain. 😜 How adventurous are you?

Sat, Jun 10, 13:34

I'm very adventurous

Sat, Jun 10, 15:34

Perfect. Do you have WhatsApp?

Yep

Cool, what's your number?

07

## Tinder

What do I want?
Her phone number!
When do I want it?
Now!

Do I really have to explain anything else?

Simplify. You are here to live a good life, so let's do it. All you need is her participation and her phone number. Then you can proceed to arranging a date on WhatsApp.

## Tinder

Wed, Oct 5, 2016, 06:51

A vegan. I must now capture you and lure you into my vegan cult.

Wed, Oct 5, 2016, 13:32

I am a free spirit. I cannae be captured.

Wed, Oct 5, 2016, 15:51

Free spirit? I hope you're a blueberry vodka then. Phone number, I want my free spirit!

Wed, Oct 5, 2016, 21:39

I'm more of a cherry vodka I'm afraid, but my number is 0

This was my first ever match on Tinder, it was also my fastest ever Tinder-to-WhatsApp conversion. Two messages, one phone number. I slept with her eventually but only met her twice.

This was not so long before I really started to structure my messages more. As you can see, what I said was based on her bio, so it is not a general thing I can use because it only applies to her.

I 'cleverly' responded to her response, and I specifically said what I want too. That is what this chapter is about after all; what you want.

I'm not even a vegan. I eat meat regularly.

I'm an entertaining person. I don't need music to keep you entertained

Yesterday • 18:27

Intriguing. Let me know when you're coming by.

I'll be there about 8. Is that ok?

Of course.

09:33

Doggy style?

19:17

So when's round 4? for you to have more of my thrilling company
Actually do you like kittens?

19:17

Today 19:27

Let's skip all the bullshit. How adventurous are you?

i am very adventurous!!

Bonus points to you! Perfect, do you have WhatsApp?

yes i do!!

+44

## SMS

As I touched upon before, SMS means 'Short Message System'. That's exactly how it should be, and that is exactly what this is all about.

Now here is a 'friend with benefits' or 'fuckbuddy', whatever you're into. She wants to come over. What do I want? I want her to, but I want to know when. So I communicate exactly that, and nothing more.

She lets me know when she will be there, I confirm it. That is all that is needed.

She then messages me again a few times after it. The perk of not messaging her back a lot is that I get to see her reveal her cards; thus I find that she wants to come back for more, and the way she communicates suggests some obsession.

## Tinder

So excited!

No messing around.

That is all it takes.

| | |
|---|---|
| Monday 20:32<br><br>Let's skip all the bullshit. How adventurous are you?<br><br>Monday 21:53<br><br>It's all relative innit. I'm in an open relationship and looking for one-time casual hook-ups on here, if you're ever in the market for that<br><br>Wonderful and straight to the point. Do you have WhatsApp?<br><br>Today 00:59<br> | **Tinder**<br><br>She knows what she wants and she is straight to the point. No **bullshit**, take it if you want it. There is absolutely nothing more to it.<br><br>She is not there to have a conversation about rainbows and pretty flowers. |
| APR 30 AT 21:29<br><br> Hahaha<br><br>Stop it!<br><br>Just tell me what happened yesterday!<br><br>APR 30 AT 22:28<br><br>I will tell you when you see me, okay? 😬<br><br>APR 30 AT 22:42<br><br> How can you do that to meeee!<br><br>And when I will see you next?<br><br>MAY 1 AT 11:21<br><br>I will do whatever I want to you. 😊 As long as we can make pancakes. 🥞<br><br>I'm gonna be available generally Monday-Thursday, as that's simply because Friday-Sunday is always crazy.<br><br>So question is, when will you see me next then? 😊 | **Facebook**<br><br>What do we want?<br>Pancakes!<br>When do we want it?<br>Now!<br><br>Evoking curiosity is often quite useful, it is like when you draw in the close attention of people you are telling an amazing story to. I hinted at telling her when I next see her, and she proceeded to ask when that would be.<br><br>I then planted a seed of an idea; pancakes, and gave a recommendation of when we should meet.<br><br>It is important to note that every message I sent here was aimed at meeting, and pointed towards arranging a time.<br><br>We started dating after this for a few months. |

Let's skip all the bullshit. How adventurous are you?

Today 11:34

The word "limit" isn't in my vocabulary

Today 14:03

Interesting. What's a good idea for our first date then? ; )

You. Me. A bed.

Fuck it come to mine and you can fuck me over my desk too

Got WhatsApp? Maybe I would prefer to fuck you on the rails of my balcony. ; )

Yeah I've got whatsapp. I'll give it to you in a bit as I'm just having a snooze. And fuck me that sounds like a good time

Today 17:50

Sure does. Now wake up and send it. ; )

Today 18:30

Hehe it's 07 **ICE   ICE**

# Tinder

Even if you run out of ideas on where to go or what to do for when you meet, you can just get any ideas she may have. This calls for her participation, making it pretty interactive in an imaginative way.

The idea a girl can give you could be amazing...

So she picked sex.

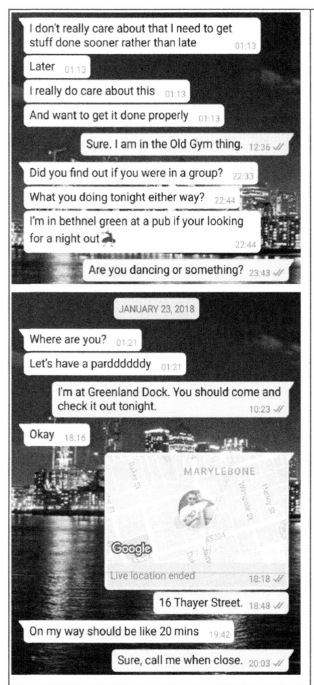

## WhatsApp

I met this girl at university and our first few messages are just some bullshit about a project.

Fast-forward to 22:33, she responds. And then 11 minutes later, she sent more messages as if she wanted me to come out with her for the night. This is a massive IOI; an indicator of interest.

It took me 59 minutes to respond to her last message that day, and then she messaged me early in the morning at 01:21, which quite clearly appears to be drunk behavior. I was sleeping.

When I woke up, I responded at 10:23. She responded vaguely at 18:17, I called her a minute later and sent my location after that. She then came and found me, and took me to a bar. I said that there's one next to my house, and she called an Uber and we went there. She paid for our food, and then we went back to my place and had sex. She stayed overnight and stayed for most of the next day.

# Common Mistakes: What Are You Doing Wrong?

Ask yourself. *'What am I doing wrong?'*

Short answer: Probably a lot, and most likely the same mistakes as everyone else. Out of the thousands of messages I have seen and have been sent from other people, there are very few people that did everything right. This isn't about perfection or comedy this is about psychology.

The first common mistake is using messages for entertainment. It is ridiculous as to how many people think that you have to entertain a girl with words in order to build her interest in you, in order to get her buying temperature high, in order to get her out with you. WRONG. That is like going up to someone o n a street and juggling, hoping to catch t heir heart and approval. You do not need to juggle or try to impress everyone you interact with. Yes, the online world can be entertaining and some memes are hilarious, but that is not going to make things happen that you need happening in your life. You're aiming to entertain her, so it will, in most cases, only lead to the possibility of ONLY entertaining her.

The second common mistake, and girls also do this, is thinking that messaging is for 'getting to know each other'. WRONG. Messaging happens on a screen. It is a completely different universe, which is why you are here right n ow reading this. You should not be telling your life story in messages to girls you meet or before you even meet. It is better to 'get to know each other' when you are both physically existing in the same geographical location. That's what people did years ago! Even if you do tell each other everything there is to know, think about what will happen when you meet; you will have less to talk about. Now imagine meeting someone you don't know too much about, they could tell you things with their voice, with their eyes, their mouth, their passion. Emotion is far superior and powerful physically; it does not exist on screens unless it is a movie or a TV show. This leads us to the next point, which is very similar. Some girls may prefer to know more about you by messaging, and that's okay. Just don't spend the next 2 months or 10 years hoping to meet and doing nothing about it.

The third common mistake is messaging without purpose or aim. Yes, you're interested in this person, but where is this going? For every message you send that does not lead you to meeting, you are wasting your time. To clarify on that, even if you have an argument with your girlfriend and you can only message her, aim to meet instead of argue. Even if arguing persists through messages, there are only two possibilities you should choose between; terminating the relationship or continuing it. If you want to continue it, you obviously picture a future where you meet. Therefore, no matter what the situation is, you always need to aim to be meeting if you're interested in someone in terms of sex or relationships. So many people are just messaging to 'get to know each other' or to say random things that are going absolutely nowhere. Now it shouldn't surprise you that it is going nowhere.

With those three points I just gave you, you now have an advantage over the majority of the planet's population because they are still going to do those things wrong, but this does not end here, we are far from done.

My personal favorite of all the mistakes people make in messaging is that of Tinder and Instagram. I will say this now - **NEVER** take messaging a girl from Tinder to Instagram. First, so many female Tinder profiles are made just to gain followers on Instagram for validation, knowing that suckers on Tinder desperately hoping to get girls will follow them and message them. Here are three of the red flags she could have mentioned in her bio:

1. *'I'm not on here much, message me on Insta @iwontfollowyouback'*
2. *'@followme'*
3. *'I don't use this, but you will have a better chance messaging me on IG @noyouwont'*

In the first case, she is just diverting you to her Instagram profile. In order to message her, you would have to follow her and then message her. On Tinder, you would have to swipe right and pray to God that she matches with you; only then can you message her on Tinder. Is it easier to message her on Instagram then? Of course. Just don't. Dozens of guys are probably just doing the same, and in many cases you won't be followed back or even have your message read by her in the first place. It's harmless to give it a try, but consider it a warning that you're just wasting your time.

In the second case, her bio contains nothing. Just her Instagram username. Nothing else. No further information. These profiles are just lazy, so quite clearly she cares more about her Instagram following than her dating life. In the third case, she also tries to divert you to Instagram while also trying to convince you that she will reply. Good luck with that, though.

Finally, in regard to going to Instagram from Tinder, some people decide to message on Tinder and then exchange Instagram profiles instead of phone numbers. Bad idea. When she gives you her phone number, you can just send her a message and that's all you need; you will then be able to meet up. However, if she gives you her Instagram profile there are things that have to happen. First, you have to follow her and then you have to wait for her to accept your request, and you might also hope for her to follow you back. There are just too many doors that she has to open for you, and that's why going to WhatsApp from Tinder is important. Never go to Instagram.

Instagram is a validation platform and you will learn more about this later on. Essentially, people just want followers, and gaining followers gives you the dopamine effect and it just validates your existence. Instagram is only about two things; likes and followers. In the dating world, girls are being offered penis from all directions. There are just too many guys trying to hit on girls, and most are absolutely sucking at it. The worst thing you can do is to put a girl on the pedestal; this means that if you keep throwing compliments at her and seem to be worshipping, praising or validating her, then you are placing her value far higher than your own. Girls love to be told they are beautiful, but when there are dozens of guys commenting on her photo saying things like *'sexy,' 'beautiful'* and trying to flirt, it's pretty creepy, and it's actually very sad.

This is an appropriate point to talk about *'Indian men on Facebook'*, a phenomenon worth looking at online for great memes and funny pictures on Google Images. As entertaining as it is, it is sad to see. It shows the reality that dozens of guys, Indian men in this case, just keep commenting the same shit or random creepy things on pictures posted by girls. Examples include, but are not limited to… *'sexy boobs'*, *'show me bobs n vagene'*, *'u luks dam beautiful'*, *'come inbox'*, or just throwing in random compliments. Think about it, do you really expect to form a relationship with a girl just because you commented on her post on Facebook? That's not how this works. There is a second but equally important question. Do you really think that a girl will fall in love with you just because you complimented her? You should be equipped with many ways of winning a girl's heart.

Furthermore, the point is that girls are receiving compliments from too many guys - guys offering dick from all sides. Guys sending pictures of their penises in the hope that they will get laid. I would like to put forward an analogy of my *'tall guy theory'*. If you are a really tall guy, you have definitely heard every comment about height before.

*'You're tall.'*
*'You must be great at basketball.'*
*'How's the weather up there?'*
*'Every time I see you, you get taller.'*
*'Stand up so I can see how tall you are.'*

*"You're tall."* If you are tall, like myself, and you hear this you may think something along the lines of *'no shit, thanks for the useless information'* even if you slightly enjoy the validation. Now when you apply the tall guy theory to girls in terms of how girls are beautiful and how guys are attracted to beauty, then it's almost exactly the same. It's great to be told you are sexy, but when lots of people are saying it you will eventually realize that everyone is just trying to fuck you. The extreme version of this on the girl's side is what I call the *'hot girl reality'*, which is discussed later on in the *"Skip The Bullshit"* chapter. To summarize, stop being like everyone else. What makes you special? What is unique about what you are saying?

## Summary

If we compile a set of rules, then this can provide you with some perspective of what you should be doing and what you should not be doing.

1. Stop building up the confidence to ask her out by trying to entertain her, you should be confident in the first place.
2. Stop trying to entertain her, everyone else is trying to.
3. Stop trying to extract life stories.
4. Stop trying to get to know each other before meeting.
5. If she prefers to message more before meeting, don't give up your ground to become pen pals with her.
6. Lead conversations with purpose. That purpose cannot be entertainment.

# Tinder

My opening line was a breath of fresh air to her because it stands out. It is different, and I'm not trying to take her out on an agenda of just sex.

My following sentences worked very well with her; I knew she had good energy and she knew I had good energy. This was because we both 'just knew' based on the fact that she admitted I made a good entrance, and that my intention was to make a good entrance anyway. In simple terms, she is responding very well to everything.

Another vital aspect of this is that she also states that I am the first guy on Tinder who is not an asshole, so that puts me way up there at the top. I am in first place.

I proceeded to get the phone number, and the next day we met and I stayed overnight at her place after watching a TV show.

I have done nothing wrong in this interaction. It worked as perfectly as it ever could, but what it tells me is that I am the only person who did not go wrong in her experience of Tinder.

**icewhiteofficial** I return in November!
#Harbour #Harbor #HarbourQueen #Ha...

 　　　　　　　　　 ⓞ **Reply**

Return London in November?

Yesterday 5:13 PM

I will be in Canada for a month.

Today 2:09 AM

And when you back

Today 1:28 PM

?

 　Replied to your story

liar

♡ Double tap to like

What did I lie about?

The marshmallow thing

I will be in London 11.19-12.11

---

## Instagram

I posted a photo on Instagram declaring that I will be flying from England to Canada in November.

This girl responded, wanting to know when I will be in London and when I won't be.

She saw my story on Instagram that showed my flight details, so she then called me a liar because she was out of London but was coming back to London to see me.

I will be back in London on 12 December.

So?

Perfect miss

It's just like you ask me to meet in Koko then you doesn't show up

Stay for longer, change your times or something.

I cannot

I have interviews after 12.10

Why don't you change urs and come back earlier or go to Canada later

I just checked my flight it's 11.19-12.10

I'm not able to change it, but I want to see you.

Why didn't you tell me the dates?

Last time I called you and I told you when I will be in London

So no you don't want to see me

I was leaving London the day before she would arrive in London. I was also returning to London the day after she was leaving. She was very upset about this.

She compared it to another time she was upset with me because she didn't find me in a club I was going to.

She wants one of us to change the travel dates so we could see each other.

I then learned that she in fact did tell me, but it was in a phone call not long before this conversation.

You are one of reasons why I stay 3 weeks in London

She was upset that she was not going to see me, when she specifically chose to stay in London for a longer time just to see me.

I'm so disappointed now

God damn. Next time you come, let me know for real.

In my mind, it would have been better if she told me not through a call but through messages. Then I would have visual of it and would not have to rely solely on memory.

I won't come to London in 2 years

Cause i will be super busy with work.

No, don't say that. There is always a way.

No I won't come for you any more

Can't trust you

She then reacts further and sends me a video of a man and woman romantically roasting marshmallows by a fire, trying to give me a picture that she wishes to spend time with me like that.

I wish it's you and me

When are you getting the apartment?

Tarnos but for now I'm living with my parents why?

Do you know when though? I never been to West France.

September maybe I will have the flat

16:26

Or you can take an rbnb if you come ahah

17:14

Okay, baby. Let's work it out. I will check transport in the next few days, you can check for some nice places to stay. Then maybe I could come and get you in a few weeks or something. ; )

The village is call Tarnos and you can take the flight from London to Anglet or Biarritz and then you can take the train to Boucau or I can come to pick you to the airport maybe if I have the car

## Facebook

This girl sends me messages after sending me messages I did not open. It means that she is more reliable than a girl who would just happily let me go. It feels good when a girl chases you, and it shows that she cares. But that's enough about pineapples.

We previously had sex, but she left the country, rendering us unable to see each other unless one travels. Even though we cannot see each other, we can at least get a picture of when the next time is. It's March, and September is 6 months away. It would be a mistake to spend the next 6 months constantly messaging each other. You will get tired of each other. So I say no more.

She chases again. She wants me to visit, proposing that we could rent a place for a few days. This means international travel is involved as well as accommodation, therefore trust is extremely important. Some of my trust is based on the fact that she is chasing me and that she really wants to see me. It would be a huge mistake if you travel somewhere far and find that she cancels or does not show up. Luckily she is not like that.

We discussed details, and my communication is clear. I said I will get back to her on it in the next few days.

She gives more information. Now the plan is in effect.

Exciting, that would be cool.

What are the first 3 things we should do? ; )

Beer bar, the beach and party in the petit Bayonne

And fooooooood

FRI AT 17:46

And for a place search on Tarnos 🙇

I then engage further imagination for what we should do in this place I have never previously visited.

Her last message here is her third time chasing in this example alone.

A week after this conversation, the flights were booked and accommodation was also arranged and paid for. When I landed, she picked me up at the airport with her dad. We had an amazing time together.

# Platforms & Social Media: Which Is Best For You?

Let's break down each type of modern communication platform. Our most common are phone numbers, WhatsApp, Facebook, Instagram and Snapchat. What you choose to do with each and which one you use the most will have a massive impact on how dating works out for you.

Phone numbers allow you to call and send messages on a network. The downside is that this costs money, and may cost additional money if you call or message phone numbers from other networks or countries. Phone numbers may also be confusing if you are new to phones. A common disadvantage is the very nature of phone numbers; it is an old system. People get new phones occasionally, or lose their phones, and quite often people change phone numbers. There is one particular story I have that made me realize how important this is. One time I met an amazing Swiss-German girl, she was stunning and I felt that she was literally perfect for me. She was wearing the best high heels, she looked beautiful and had a great style. She made moves on me. This is when I found out she had a tongue piercing. But unfortunately she was leaving the country the next day. She wanted my phone number so I added it into her phone. Little did I know that I completely messed up how I wrote the phone number because I did not put it into the international format. Because of my mistake and confusion, the difference between +44 and 07 changed everything for us, and if you don't know what this means, then that's literally all you need to be put off by phone numbers. It was quite a kick in the balls. It is a small mistake, but feels like a big mistake.

WhatsApp is pretty much just like phone numbers, only that it's Internet-based and free. You can message and call any phone number that has been set up on WhatsApp, but of course this requires an Internet connection. It has an advantage over standard network phone calls and messaging because of the fact that WhatsApp is free and that it can also show others that you have your own photo and shows you that others have their own photo too. Above that, WhatsApp also shows that messages have been delivered and read, and additionally shows when people are online. Phone numbers via WhatsApp are therefore better than phone numbers without WhatsApp. On WhatsApp, you are able to change from one phone number to another, but it does not quite solve the problem of people changing phone numbers.

Facebook is quite complex, but it is essentially the most common ongoing social network and has many advantages over WhatsApp. The first is that instead of needing a phone number to communicate with someone, you just need to know their name and you can find their profile instantly. You can send a friend request and you can message them. Becoming friends on Facebook means that you can see more of the other person's profile and they can see more of yours. The greatest thing that is underrated here is the very fact that once you become friends on Facebook, you can stay friends forever and see what everyone else is up to in their lives, and others can also see what you are doing if you post things. This is an extremely underrated advantage when it comes to connecting people to you because of the mere fact that you remain *'in touch'* and *'in contact'* without any effort or need for constant direct messaging. Phone numbers do not show you the lives people are leading, so a girl with Facebook will be able to see your life, meanwhile a girl with only y our phone number won't see anything.

Facebook profiles are literally life blogs in the form of mass messages to everyone who sees what you post. So if you post something interesting, someone you are connected with can respond and message you about it. If you were using phone numbers instead of Facebook, that person will not necessarily even know that you did something interesting. It is therefore a lost opportunity of passiveness if you primarily use phone numbers instead of social media. Every little thing you share or do on Facebook has potential. Nothing comes of most things, of course, but there is still potential. If it gets you that one extra date with someone you have not seen in a long time, then it was all worth it.

Instagram is like Facebook, but way more simplistic. Instagram is literally a photo or video sharing app, but it does not base connections on friendship, it is more of a platform for fans; there is a heavy emphasis on followers. It is therefore a validation platform. People want likes. People want comments. People want followers. Many people try to build up an Instagram profile aiming to gain lots of followers without necessarily following as many people back, but most people fail at this because they are obviously not famous or well known. Instagram is great, and perfect if you are a public figure, but essentially you are wasting a lot of time if you are trying to build your Instagram up if all you are doing to build it up is 'try to build it' and nothing else. If you have huge tits, a great ass, and post photos of yourself posing with your melons and buns on a frequent basis, then sure, you will build quite a following. But unless you have a good booty going for yourself or some external fame, you're most likely going nowhere in terms of becoming 'Instagram famous'; simply because that isn't even fame.

However, and a huge however, this does not mean you should not be using Instagram. Instagram is amazing and has great potential; just don't expect to become famous because of your unrealistic high hopes to become famous for posting a few photos. There needs to be something real to attract followers. For example, upon release of this book, perhaps I will gain Instagram popularity because of the book, not because of my Instagram posts. The source in this case is the book, not the profile. Obama and Trump would have a large following on Instagram simply because their source would be their status as leaders; the same would apply even to Hitler and Napoléon if the world had Instagram all those years ago. I'm sure everyone would love to see their content. Google, Apple and Microsoft would have a large following on Instagram not because of their posts but because you already know these companies and possibly have some of their products or like their work. But that's enough of the 'building' for now. What you need to focus on with Instagram is simply existing and posting good things, not struggling to gain fame with it when you can actually s pend that time gaining fame another way; like my aforementioned examples, becoming a politician or writing a book. You need an external source to gain significant growth, whether that is status, a big bum and breast implants, a product, a service or a business. In conclusion, stop wasting your time trying to seek massive growth on Instagram, you have to find growth outside of Instagram in order to gain growth on Instagram. Furthermore, Instagram popularity does not necessarily correlate with the amount of sexually interested girls. It is better to be followed by a few sexually interested girls than to have 100,000 followers and no sexually interested girls. Many people are not doing Instagram the right way. It is designed for fans, not friends; so don't try to grow apple trees by feeding apples to trees and don't expect that Instagram growth will be made due to a few posts you made.

On Facebook, you are friends with people. On Instagram, you follow people. If you follow someone and they do not follow back, then clearly they have a power over you; you are essentially a fan or supporter of that Instagram profile. If you follow someone and they follow you, they can unfollow at any moment, but you would still be following, perhaps not even knowing that you were unfollowed. Betrayal! It is a non-civil society of social media because it is not formed on mutual connections; it is formed of one-way bridges. If someone follows you then that's great, you have a fan. Instagram is still useful, but it is a difficult game for most people to play without the fame aspect.

Snapchat is similar to Instagram, but minus the history and minus the public view. You can only have stories that show for 24 hours and then disappear forever. You have no profile. You have no timeline. No history. Snapchat is a completely different story, but in simple terms, Instagram is far superior and far more beneficial. There is a chapter dedicated to Snapchat to give further insight on that case, so we will put Snapchat to the side for now because it is not quite as significant as Instagram or Facebook in this comparison, and because it is more of a unique case.

Let's break it all down into a few aspects.

## Communication Types

The table below shows the 3 most useful elements of how we communicate on each platform. Phone numbers and WhatsApp are very much one-to-one interactions, but social media enables you to send messages in other forms like stories or posts. People can easily interact with you if you make a post or a story, and likewise you can also quite easily interact with other people based on what they share. Stories appear for 24 hours and then disappear, allowing contacts, friends or followers to see photos and videos that you would like to share. Facebook profiles have a timeline, which effectively go back to the day you were born. Instagram profiles also have a form of this timeline, only that it is for photos and videos only and not just words.

|  | Phone | WhatsApp | Facebook | Instagram | Snapchat |
|---|---|---|---|---|---|
| Messaging | ✓ | ✓ | ✓ | ✓ | ✓ |
| Stories | X | ✓ | ✓ | ✓ | ✓ |
| Timelines | X | X | ✓ | ✓ | X |

## Ease of Interaction

Due to the nature of social media, it therefore means that social media allows passivity. Interaction via phone numbers and WhatsApp are extremely limited because they only allow direct communication between you and individuals. You can have group chats on WhatsApp, of course, but that is highly irrelevant unless you are hosting orgies or something.

|         | Phone | WhatsApp | Facebook | Instagram | Snapchat |
|---------|-------|----------|----------|-----------|----------|
| Direct  | ✓     | ✓        | ✓        | ✓         | ✓        |
| Passive | X     | X        | ✓        | ✓         | ✓        |

## Regarding Time

Anything by default can be potentially short term. However, it is natural for interactions through phone, WhatsApp and Snapchat to be very temporary when compared to Facebook and Instagram; Facebook keeps you connected for the rest of your life, and Instagram also allows your posts to exist forever. The long-term aspect of both Facebook and Instagram are due to their use of timelines and profiles. At any moment, a week from now, a month from now, 5 years from now, anyone with access to your Facebook profile or Instagram profile can interact with you or your posts; you have a history. Phone and WhatsApp messages stay, but nobody reminisces the past of messages; apart from me for the purpose of writing this book of course. Snapchat is a platform surrounded with the theme of disappearing; even the logo is a ghost, and ghosts disappear. Nothing on Snapchat lasts beyond the day after something was shared, which makes it extremely short term.

Short term is useful for the present. Long term is useful for the future.

|            | Phone | WhatsApp | Facebook | Instagram | Snapchat |
|------------|-------|----------|----------|-----------|----------|
| Short Term | ✓     | ✓        | ✓        | ✓         | ✓        |
| Long Term  | X     | X        | ✓        | ✓         | X        |

## Connection Types

Now let's separate fans and friends. You can have followers on Facebook, Instagram and Snapchat. Out of all your followers on Instagram and Snapchat, you can choose to follow some back, but this connection does not count as friendship in this case because the digital relationship is built on two one-way bridges; you following them and them following you. Facebook, therefore, is the only major platform that allows you to have friends, because it is a digital relationship that is easier to maintain, partially due to the fact that the 'fans and followers' mentality on Instagram and Snapchat lead to a lot of unfollowing as a result of the ego. Facebook is thus more sustainable.

Fans are useful for having some kind of support. Friends are useful for maintaining relationships and life-long support.

|         | Phone | WhatsApp | Facebook | Instagram | Snapchat |
|---------|-------|----------|----------|-----------|----------|
| Fans    | X     | X        | ✓        | ✓         | ✓        |
| Friends | X     | X        | ✓        | X         | X        |

## Location Types

This part is not massively important, but still quite interesting. Your own location can be shared on WhatsApp, Facebook, Instagram and Snapchat. WhatsApp and Facebook allow you to share your live location. Facebook and Instagram allow you to share the location of a post. For example, if I post on Facebook and Instagram a picture of me at the Hard Rock Cafe in Los Angeles, then people can see that I have been there and possibly respond to it; I can also see via Facebook any friends that have also shared their experience at that location. Facebook and Instagram are also extremely useful with stories too, you can tag the location of where you were, and this is the best way of getting reactions and responses from viewers of your story; it has personally led me to quite a lot of dates from this feature alone. Snapchat is on a different level, and allows you to view a map of the world and see where your friends are, it is especially useful in the sense that it is very simple and easy to see if you will cross paths with someone or find that someone you are connected to is nearby.

Locations are useful in that even the dumbest people can figure out, or at least use the technology's directions to do the work for them, where they need to go if they are meeting someone.

|  | Phone | WhatsApp | Facebook | Instagram | Snapchat |
|---|---|---|---|---|---|
| **Post Location** | X | X | ✓ | ✓ | X |
| **Send Location** | X | ✓ | ✓ | X | X |
| **Live Location** | X | ✓ | ✓ | X | ✓ |
| **Live Map** | X | X | X | X | ✓ |

Think about how some of these features may benefit you. When Facebook first introduced the stories feature, I instantly judged it as a copy of Instagram and refused to use it or look at it. Months later, I eventually tried it and it has ever since served good use. Long-term platforms are also important if you w ant to consider maximizing or maintaining your connections without any direct effort.

## Summary

Which platform is the winner? Which platform are people using the most? Which platform is the most beneficial?

I conducted a poll to find out which platforms men, those who were serious about this stuff, were using the most when they were meeting girls and wanted to stay in touch. The question was 'what is your preferred method of closing?' this 'closing' term refers to acquiring someone's contact details consensually. For example, if a girl gives you her phone number, that is called a number-close; then you will be able to message her on your phone or call her, or message her on WhatsApp. If she gives you her Instagram username, then you have then closed her on Instagram once you have followed each other on Instagram. If she gives you her Facebook profile, then you have Facebook-closed her. It is important to note, however, that it is not a number-close if you gave her your phone number, and it is not closing if you just gave her your details for Instagram, Facebook or so on. It is only closing if the accurate information has been consensually given to you.

## Points scored

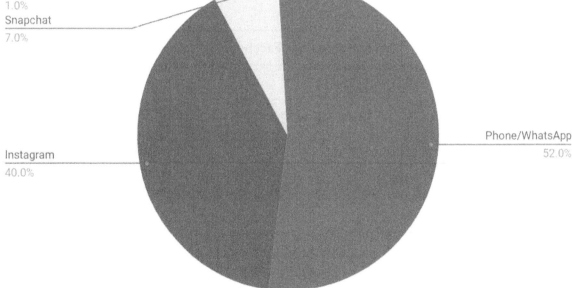

Facebook
1.0%
Snapchat
7.0%

Instagram
40.0%

Phone/WhatsApp
52.0%

The findings from the poll were interesting but I was personally not surprised by the outcome. 52% of those studied said that they primarily try to number-close or to exchange phone numbers so that they could message on their phone or through WhatsApp. 40% of those studied said that they primarily attempt to follow girls on Instagram, while 7% of those studied use Snapchat to stay connected with girls they meet. Only 1% use Facebook.

However, this does not mean that Facebook is the worst and that WhatsApp is the best. Based on what each platform offers as features, Facebook is in fact the most beneficial. There is simply one concept which can justify this alone and it is called the six degrees of separation. This is a theory that all people are 6 or fewer social connections away from each other. It is a chain comparable to the 'a friend of a friend' phrase. It is the idea that everything is connected, and this power of the six degrees of separation is of extreme significance because Facebook holds the ability to show you not only how many mutual friends you have with someone, but who these mutual friends are. So imagine how powerful it is when you meet someone who already knows someone you know. It is actually a  lot more likely than you may think. As a personal example, I once met a New Yorker in London who was in the same university class in New York as someone who knew me from a completely different setting, and we only knew this because Facebook told us that the connection is there. I also dated a Portuguese woman that had multiple Facebook friends, who had mutual friends with me on Facebook. On top of this, two people who followed me on Instagram pointed out that they know her; one worked with her and one was Portuguese. I met the person who worked with her, but not the second person. I never set foot in Portugal. I never met this woman through friends of my own.

Facebook's data team documented in 2011 that among the 721 million users, there were 69 billion friendship links and an average distance of 4.74 degrees of separation, and that **99.91% of all Facebook users were interconnected.** In 2016, it was then reported to have been reduced to 4.57 at 1.6 billion users, meaning that we are now even more connected than before. I personally have mutual friends on Facebook with various public figures, as well as direct friendships with others; which in theory makes me massively more able to gain access to such people. In a similar version known as 'six degrees of Kevin Bacon', there is also the data supporting that you can link so many different actors based on movies they have appeared in. For example, Kevin Bacon was in The Big Picture with Eddie Albert; who starred in Brother Rat with Ronald Reagan. You can do your own searches and it is crazy that so many things are interconnected in a minimal number of degrees.

In the movie *The Social Network,* based on the true story of how Facebook was created, there was a scene where Zuckerberg feels like he is missing something from the website. He realized it was the relationship status feature; this is a feature that many other apps do not have. It's useful for screening who is single and who is not.

I thus emphasize that Facebook should be used a lot more when closing. When you establish a connection on Facebook, you establish a connection with endless potential for further connections, mutual connections and more connections. Although Instagram has a similar feature of seeing that a profile is followed by people you follow, the Instagram connection system's use of followers instead of friends makes it far less connected and far less visible for a large variety of reasons. Instagram is therefore less secure than Facebook in terms of maintaining connections. One being that you may be Facebook friends with your mom, but you probably don't follow her on Instagram.

Other bonus points that Facebook achieves are that people can like your photos and you can like other people's content. If you connect with a girl you like on Facebook, she can like your photos. Each new connection you make on Facebook or Instagram, male or female, is a connection that can contribute towards your social proof levels by supporting what you post; liking pictures, statuses and videos. When that girl likes your photos on Facebook or even on Instagram, it is an IOI; indicator of interest. Receiving likes can quite often tell you who is responding to your posts well, and thus they obviously think pretty well of you and like you as a person. When your mom likes your photo, that's family love. When your best friend likes your photos consistently, that's friendly support. When a girl you like likes your photos consistently, that's an IOI. This all gives you information as to who likes what you are doing or what you are posting. Every single friend, follower or like gained contributes to your social proof on social media. It all adds up, and it will certainly build up long term.

I would then rank Instagram as second, but this is also not to say that other platforms, such as WhatsApp, are of no use. All people you meet in a social sense should ideally be connected through social media instead of WhatsApp. The only exception to this is when you find someone from Tinder, or other dating platforms, by which I maintain that those you interact with on Tinder should be connected with on WhatsApp. Definitely do not migrate an interaction from Tinder to Instagram, and certainly not from Tinder to Facebook. WhatsApp first in the case of Tinder. You can make an exception for Facebook if she decides it would be better to connect on Facebook, but this is rare. The problem of taking an interaction from Tinder to Instagram is the problem of ego, validation and the massive personal incentive for girls to get as many followers as possible from dumb guys who will just follow her orders and follow her on Instagram and like her photos.

Facebook and Instagram allow you to easily orchestrate **DHV**. This means *demonstration of higher value*. However, Instagram can easily be exploited by girls to provide a DHV, because every thirsty guy will just follow her and like all her posts in the hope that he will be noticed by her. Instagram is a powerful DHV if you have achieved an optimal set up.

| | Facebook | Instagram | Other |
|---|---|---|---|
| **Social Proof** | ✓ | ✓ | X |
| **Passive** | ✓ | ✓ | X |
| **Long Term** | ✓ | ✓ | X |
| **Timelines** | ✓ | ✓ | X |
| **Mutual Connections** | ✓ | ✓ | X |
| **Friends** | ✓ | X | X |

# Skip The Bullshit: How Do You Take Her Out?

So ask yourself. *'How do I take her out?'*

Forget everything you thought you knew.

Imagine for a moment that you are a girl. Girls have vaginas. And boobs. Everyone likes vaginas and boobs, right? Right. Now imagine that you are a girl with Facebook, Instagram and Tinder. Guys are messaging you everywhere, even commenting on everything you post. Your reality is different t o a man's reality because you have way too much choice than you even asked for. There's too much dick in your face! You have dozens of messages sent to you on Facebook and Instagram on a regular basis. You have hundreds of potential matches waiting for you to accept on Tinder. This is the *hot girl reality*. How can she sift through all the bullshit?

Let's touch back on your personal Tinder experience. It is an undeniable fact that you swipe right based on attractiveness, primarily in physical attractiveness, and secondary is perhaps something you like that you saw in their description or a photo. Every once in a while, you see an overweight girl o r a transgender. I do not consider myself an expert on transgender issues, but most transgenders that you come across in any way are male to female. They also tend to really exaggerate their femininity. Why is that? My personal theory that is only based on observation is that some males question their sexuality or gender if they struggle in attracting females, and because they so desperately are attracted to females but cannot satisfy their need, they choose to *'change to female'* because that way they could potentially see themselves as attractive. Therefore, they go all out on trying to be female, especially in how they tend to dress, move or use makeup.

Females have validation everywhere they go in terms of attractiveness. I might be exceptionally handsome myself, but I only get catcalled on the streets every few years. Jokes aside, this is relevant because things are straightforward in what you want. You probably don't want someone who is fat. You also probably don't want to match with a man disguising himself as a woman. What you want is a physically attractive woman. Moreover, because that is what you want, it is what nearly all other men want. So you're kinda fucked, because every girl you find attractive is every girl you swipe right on, and everyone else is doing that. Many guys are swiping left of profiles of overweight girls or transgenders, so if you swipe right on every profile, you most likely will match with overweight girls or transgenders. The Tinder algorithm will screw you over if y our swiping is not based on your own authentic standards.

Now imagine being a really hot girl. Based on the *'hot girl reality'* I have witnessed, there's an even more ridiculous a mount to it. Hundreds of people are sending you messages on Instagram alone in the space of two weeks. You have lots of Facebook messages, and thousands of potential matches. There was a famous case in 2018; a woman known as Natasha Aponte invited hundreds of her Tinder matches in New York to Union Square in Manhattan and stood on a stage to weed out the men according to whether or not they have a beard or support Donald Trump as President of the United States. A man has never had this power on Tinder, because men are not high in demand despite the female population being higher than the male population. So something is going wrong. This is the imbalance of dating.

One of those reasons is pretty simple. Men are generally attracted to exactly the same things. In caveman words; *'boobs, vagina, face'*. What women want is confused not only by the insanely unnecessary amount of choice, but the complications that come with it. A woman can like a man for his personality, but you cannot see personality just by looking. A man can see that something is attractive just by looking. In the simplest terms, what men want is far simpler than what women want. A man is not going to get many messages or matches on Tinder unless there is really something about him, such as fame.

So your main problem is that, as a man, you are competing with everyone else. To most guys, it is hard to win. But this doesn't mean you should give up on girls and turn gay or jump off a bridge, this can actually become something in your favor too even if that is hard to believe. If most guys are competing against each other for a girl, every single one of them loses if they are the same as everyone else. **Your advantage is the opportunity to be different, and that is how you can come out on top with your own sexual value.**

If you can accurately show who you are as a person, you have already won. Nobody can be you better than you can. The biggest failure of many profiles, especially on Tinder, is when the profile is made by a man who doesn't quite understand who he is as a person yet. If you don't know who and what you are, she sure as hell won't know. Many girls have a better idea about who they are, because f or them it is a bit simpler. Many girls want to be attractive, and they want to convey that. They know men are attracted to beauty, and they really care about how they look. What do they do about it? They buy over $500 billion USD of cosmetic products. Some even undergo surgery to get bigger boobs and bigger buttcheeks. However, men do not truly know how to be attractive in general, and you couldn't really identify an industry comparable to the cosmetic industry that males would spend so much money on to make themselves attractive. What is attractive about a man is the fact that he knows what he wants, knows who he is, and knows how to express himself authentically. Everything you do, especially how you communicate, reveals information about who you are and how you feel about yourself. If this book was written out of uncertainty, you would not be confident in my writing and you would not have made it to this page.

Now, let's look back into a girl's phone. What kind of messages is she receiving by these random thirsty men on the Internet? Pictures of dicks. Boring messages of *'how are you?'* and *'I like your photo'*. Messages filled with complete bullshit. Most people go nowhere with messages like these because everyone else is saying the same shit. Even if some of these guys do slip through the cracks, they fall down at the next hurdles because they are like dogs chasing cars; they would not know what to do if they ever did catch one. As aforementioned, the guys who did not get ignored tend to be shut down by their next moves because they either lack purpose or are not getting to the point. Some people think that sending a picture of your own dick is the way of getting to the point. What does sending a picture of your dick do anyway? If she wants to see it, she can meet you and take a peek herself, which I believe is the reason you are trying to message her anyway. You are attracted to females because you are biologically designed to have sex with them. In order for that to happen, you need to actually meet them. But before we get to meeting them, how do we find them?

Tinder has three options for you to decide who to match - swiping left, swiping right or using a superlike. I will address the latter first. A very common question asked about Tinder was about superlikes and whether or not they should be used. Should you superlike someone? If you superlike someone, isn't it needy? Tinder provides you with very few superlikes each week and depending on your Tinder membership you could have 1 per day or even 5. It is **not** needy to use a superlike. I have in fact used it myself many times and dated a model long term because of it. To refuse to use it is to lose an opportunity.

In consideration of superlikes, don't hand out your superlike to someone just because you think they are attractive, 50 other guys probably did the same for that same person. You should superlike if you find her relatively attractive and if her bio or photo has something extremely relatable to you. For example, I superliked a girl because one of her photos had my friend in the background. I won't find that every day, so it is particularly special. Another example is if I just returned from France and Spain and there is a girl who is half-French and half-Spanish, it is a good opportunity to superlike. If it is relatable to you and you are superliking her for that, then you have a better chance because other people will not be superliking her for the same reason. Do not superlike her if her profile says she is only visiting for a few days.

As for swiping, do not s wipe right all the time. You will be ranked poorly by Tinder and your matches will most likely be low quality and infrequent. I personally only swipe right on profiles that have at least three photos clearly of her, and if none of those photos have stupid Snapchat filters. I do not want to date a girl who is so bored that she decided to take a picture of herself as a dog as if she is 14 years old. I swipe left on non-female profiles. I swipe left if there are Snapchat filters. I swipe left if her profile tells me she is only interested in classy people. I swipe left is her photos show that she only likes to dress up in a classy way and is not even happy in those photos. I decide whom I want to match with based on how good she looks, how many photos she has and how positive she seems. Boredom, no emotion and no personality are turn offs. If they are turn offs for me, they must also be turnoffs for others; it goes both ways. So it is also important to consider how someone may judge you.

This chapter is about skipping the bullshit; the name of the chapter is inspired by the original line that came to be known as the **spontaneous line**. It was popularized from the original Message Game Guide (2018) that I created. Only one tiny change to the opener was made since I started using it. I have been using the **adventurous line** since 2018. What hasn't changed is the bullshit skipping. In Message Game philosophy, it is extremely important to skip the bullshit. Anything that doesn't take a step towards meeting is called bullshit. Every message you send that does not attempt to solve problems to get to meeting her is bullshit. **Anything without purpose is bullshit.** The purpose is to meet her. If you are asking her about her day, that's bullshit. That is not taking a step to meeting her.

There are three official Message Game lines I have created over time. These lines were created by myself, and it took time to understand why they work pretty well. Will they work on every girl? No. But they will certainly help you out in many interactions and give you some good chances.

## The Spontaneous Line

*'Let's skip all the bullshit. How spontaneous are you?'*

I started using this line in 2017. I don't even know what gave me the idea, but I gave up on the openers I was using before, which were absolutely useless and achieved nothing. The reason the spontaneous line worked so well is because it comes out of nowhere into a girl's messages and tells her that you won't give her annoying or unnecessary bullshit or useless messages. It also asks a question which screens her first, instead of her screening you. Thus, this gives you a power position of controlling the conversation easily even if you don't understand message game dynamics. Because of the screening, it is as if you are testing her, which sets a change of your position from inferior, which many guys fall into, to superior. When a teacher gives you a test, you will pass or f ail. The teacher is thus superior for testing you, regardless of whether you passed or not. This line was featured many times in the original Message Game Guide (2018), and for well over a year people started using it. By the time I finished the guide, I stopped using it and switched to the next line. This was the only frequent line I used, and the only one featured in the guide.

## The Adventurous Line

*'Let's skip all the bullshit. How adventurous are you?'*

I started using this line in 2018. I felt that *'adventure'* is a better word than *'spontaneity'* and could open up to a lot more potential. The only difference is literally that one word changed. This opener was never made public until this book was released, but I was using it while every follower of Message Game was using the spontaneous line. Like the aforementioned spontaneous line, this screens her. However, this also tells you, via how she responds, how fun she is. If she doesn't respond well, she isn't very fun. If she responds well, that's perfect. At least you now have more information as to whether or not you will get along. I realized months later that this is powerful because, out of the thousands of female Tinder profiles I looked at, I understood that there were patterns. Lots of girls had the word *'adventure'* in their bio. This was just one of many patterns I noticed.

## The 3 Things Line

*'Can you name 3 things that would be amazing for a date?'*
*'Can you name 3 things you wanna do on our first date?'*
*'Tell me 3 things you want to do if we meet.'*

This line is actually fresher than this book itself. I came up with this line not long after I started writing this book. It works well because it gives her the cue to tell you what she wants. And as simple as that, you know what she wants because she literally told you. Message game is much more straightforward than it may seem. She can then name 3 things and you can meet up and do at least one. This also often returns responses about sex, so it cuts through the bullshit extremely well.

Stop wasting time with your bullshit, all that is going to do is complicate things.

You also need to be the man. Girls are not going to do all the work for you, they don't know this shit. If they can't remember where they put their phone and keep losing their hair clips, how can you expect them to take control and decide things for you? You have to lead. Never tell her *'let me know'*. She's probably not leading a life that is so organized that she has the time, courtesy and memory to come back to you when she is ready to *'let you know'* about what is good or when is good. To meet a woman, you need three things. Here is a comprehensive list of those things:

1. A woman
2. A place
3. A time

Ideally, you already have a woman. If you don't, go find one. Then you need a place and a time to meet. There could be no simpler explanation. The place needs to be relatively easy for both of you to get to, so the Moon is not a good idea. A good idea is something near to you, and ideally she should be comfortable meeting you there and able to easily travel there. This gives you good **logistics.** Some girls will not be comfortable coming straight to your house unless you have already agreed to cook, watch a movie, have drinks or have sex. If she is not comfortable coming straight to your place, that doesn't mean she cannot end up at your place. You can arrange to meet at a place like a restaurant, a park, a bar or whatever else you could choose. Most girls I have arranged to meet with that did not want to come straight to my place actually ended up at my place anyway, even after just 2 hours.

To make something go somewhere with a girl, you have to stop being a girl and start being a man. Feminization and suppression of masculine traits in society in recent years have caused a lot of social awkwardness and confusion between males and females. Many males are lost when it comes to life choices and especially dating, and that is possibly because of the suppression of masculinity in society today.

Take her out. No more bullshit, cut out the unnecessary shit and just take steps towards the goal of taking her out. You should be the one in control and you should be the one leading and setting the frame. You should be the one to define the relationship, not waiting for her to accept you or choose you.

You choose her.

Hey

What's your job exactly? Sounds super interesting

Do you talk about google's tech&research on tv or something?

Sunday 16:37

Well, damn. I'm a Googler. I handle events and marketing, and I talk in events, meetings, etc inside and outside of Google.

For Google I talk about developments in hardware and the software that comes with it, but I am also put on panels about random other things, and work with a lot of technology startups that are associated with Google For Entrepreneurs.

I have to refuse talking on TV or the media because I can only do that when Google wants me to, and Google prefers to reveal everything via Google (AKA, the Internet) itself.

But I have spoke about non-Google things.

Sunday 21:37

Oh, i was wondering why google had such low media coverage. So they try to avoid it.

What did u study at uni? How did you find such an interesting job? 😃 you are my inspiration Alex ice 😃

Sunday 22:37

My name is Ice.

## Tinder

She was more interested in my job role than anything else.

We actually had genuine conversations, and I invited her to an event I was speaking at. She attended, but we never spoke face to face. It could have been a pretty cool love story, but at least it was a unique experience. She saw me up there, but I probably never saw her in the room.

It's a long story. Do you have WhatsApp? I am speaking at a public Google event on Tuesday.

...day 23:53

07...

Instead of answering a million more questions in paragraphs, I decided to move it to WhatsApp as well as specify that there is an event she could meet me at.

No bullshit.

---

Today 22:54

I just wanted to say... I saw the background of your photo saying 'Antics'. I'm there every week and one of my photos is also from it. You going again any time soon?

hi... you mean in Koko? I've been there a few times but I don't have anything planned to come again

Sure. I love it. You should come on Friday next week (24). Do you have WhatsApp?

I can't make it because I've got an exam that sat and have to get ready for it

+44...

**Tinder**

This makes me sad but also happy.

Because of these two messages, I went on to meet this girl and took her out to the place I was referring to, which was a club night.

She was a model. We went on to date for a few months and we had an amazing time together and many adventures, we even travelled thousands of miles together.

Unfortunately, it ended after nearly 6 months.

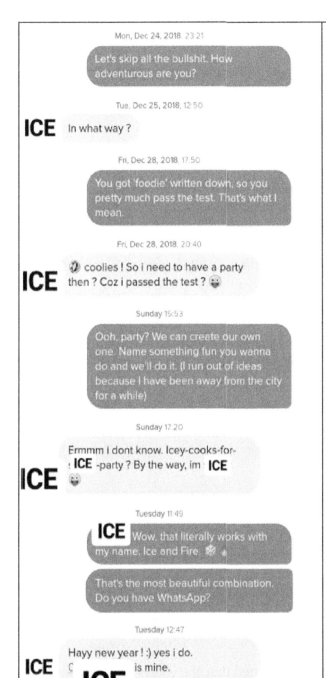

## Tinder

She wanted to know what I meant, so I referred to her bio to skip the explanation. I then wait for her response.

She responded well, so I used this to proceed further into arranging an activity, and then receiving her phone number.

Her name is not Fire, by the way. But our similar opposites were a good opportunity to make this seem like we have to take it further.

We had a series of adventures on the day we met and started seeing each other more. We had a very good sexual relationship.

**ICE** Will you go to koko this Friday

00:09

I'm gonna be flying somewhere. Meet me tomorrow.

**ICE** Yeah then you ask me to meet at somewhere and don't show up

Won't be like that. I'll make you a deal. I can even share my location or you can just meet me at my place. I can give you a tour of my area. Deal?

Your place?

**ICE** Where

09:59

Greenland Dock.

**ICE**

Ok

**ICE** See you around 1pm. Ok?

Alrighty, I'll be here.

**ICE** But what we do

Whatever we want. I got some ideas.

**ICE** Anyway I'm not coming for hook up.

Oh, no. You gotta date me 3 times before I even let you touch me.

**ICE** Don't be mean

---

**SMS**

She wanted to know if we would meet at a place, I regularly go to. I was genuinely going to be somewhere else, so I gave her a different option.

She was insecure or worried about me potentially not showing up; therefore, the solution is to let her know that there is nothing to worry about. To solve this, I suggested that I could share my live location so she knows exactly where I am.

She was curious about the idea, and I gave her my address because I was at home.

At 11:21 she said she would be there at 13:00; that is 99 minutes away. Because she decided to come so spontaneously, she is quite clearly very interested in me.

She also stated that she was not coming to have sex. Classic **shit test**!

I responded with a joke in response to her saying that we will not have sex. Reacting to it will cause a problem and show her that I am just interested in sex, even if it is not true.

| | |
|---|---|
| Deal with it. Wear something cute, so we match. ; ) | She turned up exactly 90 minutes later and despite saying that she did not want to have sex, she started being sexual shortly after she arrived. |
| **ICE** I have nothing cute | |
| So wear nothing. ; ) | |
| **ICE** Hey!<br>Got back last night and just getting out of the gym<br>How are you?<br><br>13:06<br><br>I'm wonderful, lots of funny things catching my amusement.<br><br>13:36<br><br>**ICE** Hahaha good to hear!<br>So what are you doing tonight?<br><br>13:57<br><br>Well I was hoping you would join me in Little Canada. ; )<br><br>Where's that?<br><br>And what is it?<br><br>I don't think I have your number... let's whatsapp instead? I don't use this so **ICE** much 07 ☺ ICE | **Facebook**<br><br>Be grateful when a girl makes the moves on you. Not only is it easier to understand their intentions, it is also easier as a whole because you know there is interest of some form. Confidence is key.<br><br>These messages were all simple and straightforward, and the next steps had us go out together. |

Today 14:48

Let's skip all the bullshit. How adventurous are you?

Today 15:22

Depends what kind of adventures you are talking about?

Although from your photo I'm guessing you are looking for adventures of the sexual kind so that's probably not for me and so you can feel free to unmatch me

**ICE**

Today 16:30

That's just a photoshoot, it has nothing to do with sex, it's just sexy. I would like to think all of my pictures are. ;)

Generally I like trying new food, anything interesting.

Now anything involving new food is my kind of thing.

In terms of adventures - first dates can be so dull. If it was just a drink in a bar, I'd probably score myself a 3/10

If it was doing something random like go ape, skating, a bungee jump, an escape room, an assault course then that would be far more interesting

**ICE** However, I totally get that that is not most peoples idea of a fun first date

What you just said is literally everything I believe in, that's exactly what I want. Coffee is so boring, that's just sitting down and talking about our life stories. We really need to actually live.

You nailed it. Go Ape or skating would be great, I haven't done the first one.

**ICE** So let's go ape!

**Tinder**

A few back and forth messages solidified the date and the phone number.

First, she was a little alarmed by one of my photos, which was a photo of me looking at the camera while a girl is wearing high heels and has her legs on me. To her it is just something she needs to test me on, all I have to do is pass the test; I did so by explaining it a little and making a joke out of it, and then addressing what I actually meant and what I actually want out of the implications of my first message to her.

Her view on dating was exactly like my view on dating. Towards the end, I received her phone number and we solidified a fun date for a few days later.

We did not actually do this, we chose something else.

| | |
|---|---|
| I'm amazed. Perfect, that's it then. Do you have WhatsApp?<br><br>Sure 07 **ICE ICE**<br><br>**ICE** I'm free Sunday afternoon from 3 - let me see what I can find and I'll book it | Say no more. It's done. |

TUE AT 20:39

You are now connected on Messenger.

TUE AT 23:42

> Happen to know a good place in London for a white guy to get Jollof rice? 😂

WED AT 00:42

I've actually never been to an African restaurant so I wouldn't know 😕

But I want to go to one so hopefully I'll come up with a good suggestion

WED AT 13:54

> Wow, guess I'm winning then. I just found one in Canning Town, wanna check it out on Friday?

WED AT 14:06

Yeah that would be great I wouldn't mind

WED AT 14:21

> Cool, where do you live by the way? Just so I know where it's best to meet.

I live in Wembley Park so I can just meet you at Canning Town if it's easier

WED AT 14:43

> You can meet me at Canada Water, which is on the way to it anyway. Is 17:40 at Canada Water good?

Yeah that's cool

## Facebook

We met on this day, and we became friends on Facebook. We were at a small university event, and I intrigued her the moment we met. It turned out that she had the same name as my ex-girlfriend and came from the same place as her.

Asking for a good place for a standard Nigerian food choice, it was opportunistic to take her along with me to a Nigerian restaurant knowing that she has never had that experience.

A time and rough location was specified.

For logistical reasons, I later checked where she would be travelling from, so that we could meet before getting to the location itself; my area was in between her area and where we were going.

The day before the date, the time and meeting place was solidified.

WED AT 15:41

Perfect, see you there. And be hungry, because the portions are quite insane. 😊

WED AT 19:25

Great! I'm always hungry 😊

THU AT 22:31

Perfection. I shall see you again tomorrow. 17:40, Canada.

FRI AT 16:07

You ready? 😊

Definitely 😊

FRI AT 16:43

Cool. Let me know when you reach.

I'm here

On the day of meeting, I checked for her to be ready nearly two hours before the meeting time since she did not respond, this is to double-confirm not only that she would be making it but also to confirm that the plan has not changed and that she would be on time.

We ate Nigerian food and I puked onto my plate.

But still, I took her home with me.

## Tinder

Let's skip all the bullshit. How adventurous are you?

**ICE** How adventurous are you?

> You first. ; )

**ICE** Hah I don't know have to define it...

> I guess a better question is... Name 3 things... ANYTHING. We should probably do for our first date, then we may have to do at least one.

Hot air balloon 🎈

**ICE** Now you go...

> Ooh, romantic already.

> Bake cookies and force feed them to each other like besties and watch a movie.

> Your turn. ; )

Take a little boat out on a lake in a park, then drink prosecco on the grass

**ICE** Your go

> That's perfect. Travel to another country in Europe just for a few days for the hell of it.

Ahh a city break

**ICE** So which one...?

> Let's get a boat. I like that

Perfect!

**ICE** I've never actually done that

> Neither have I, but it seems amazing. I have plenty of Prosecco. Do you have WhatsApp?

Today 23:02

**ICE** I do have what's app 07 **ICE ICE**

---

**Tinder**

Using my opener, I did not get an answer from her; instead, she asked me the same question without giving me an answer first.

She wanted some definition, so I planted the fun idea of using her imagination to do something amazing for a date.

She named something, I named something. We repeated this. The idea of making cookies and feeding them to each other seems very innocent and girly, but it's just supposed to be a fun idea to capture her creativity and emphasize the fact that we could do pretty much whatever we want. However, the main reason is different. Where can you bake cookies, watch a movie and escalate sexually with her all in one location? At your own place.

Then we chose the most amazing one, and moved onto WhatsApp.

---

When and where would u want to meet then 21:45

TODAY

I found a cool place, but times for Sundays won't work for me. Saturday or Monday works for me. Everything looks so good! 15:17

It's around Covent Garden. 15:18

What is the place called ? 15:34

Gotta copy and paste, it's pretty complicated. 17:09

Choccywoccydoodah. I'm not making this up. ; ) 17:09

Oh i know there ! I mean i have passed by but didnt know they have a cafe ! 17:17

What about tuesday 17:18

I passed by too but didn't know. Tuesday is perfect. 17:26

What about the time. 17:26

I can make it after 4 17:27

That's good, let's do your earliest time, that works out neatly. 17:29

## WhatsApp

She did not want to eat out on the first date and instead suggested coffee. I don't like coffee and see coffee dates as boring, so before this screenshot I called upon going to a cool hot chocolate place. Time and date was set.

We then met that day for our first date, and she paid for it. We then went to explore the nearby streets and headed to a landmark area of the city to sit on the stairs for a while. I then offered to cook together at my place, so we went home to cook; so it turned out that we did eat together on our first date.

After all this, she stayed over and we slept together.

Today 16:41

Let's skip all the bullshit. How adventurous are you?

Well I could be a little better

**ICE** What do you have in mind?

I wanna know 3 practical things you have in mind, things you need or want to do since you need more. ; )

**ICE** You can't answer my question with a question!

It wasn't a question. My answer is that what is on my mind is wondering what you have in mind. Silly. ; )

😬 ok fine

**ICE** I don't have much on my mind tbh

In that case, just pick out a few things we should do from my random ideas. Or anything you think of in inspiration.

Milkshakes, pillow fight, waffles, movie, cooking. (Can you cook?)

Pillow fight 😬

**ICE** No I can't cook

Well that's a deal. I'll probably want food as well, so we shall see. Got WhatsApp?

Today 19:04

Yeah 0: **ICE ICE**

But I can't do tonight

**ICE** I'm feeling shitty now, feeling jet lagged and hungover 😬

---

**Tinder**

Line sent.

She answers, but she responds with a question; she is curious and wants to know more.

Plant the seed of meeting by introducing exciting ideas. A tiny bit of playfulness, but she does not have any ideas.

Time for inspiration. I sent her some ideas to pick so I could spark some excitement or imagination.

Transfer to WhatsApp; job done. She also mentions that she is not able to do today, which means that if she was able then she would have jumped right on the opportunity. I do not tend to match with someone and then meet them on the same day, but this is good information.

We baked cookies and had sex.

---

Have I? Oh ur flatmates ? 17:41

Haha i get it :) u said ur Russian girlfriends so I thought someone flew over to London :) 17:42

Time and location? 17:42

My house. I will be home from 18:30. The place is a street away from the house so when they are ready we can all go. 18:03

TODAY

Cool :) Then I will do my best to find ur house 😂 specific time u want to me arrive at? 07:34

19:30 is good. 10:52

ok :) any dress code? 😂 14:01

Dress sexy. ; ) 15:18

Well, anything. It's just food, so no big deal. 15:18

I am no where close to 'sexy' mode 🙃 I will do my best tho😊 16:46

I know. ; ) 17:32

## WhatsApp

Arranging a third date. My idea was for her to join me and two Russian female friends of mine at a place near my house for food.

One of my friends was held up at work, so I arranged something for the future with my two friends. Meanwhile, the girl from this interaction came and just the two of us went there.

We got on very well and we discussed deep things, and we even talked happily about the fact that my relationships often involve multiple girls.

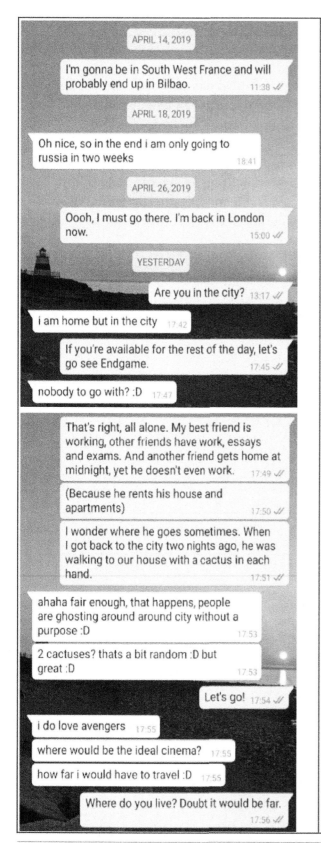

## WhatsApp

We did not message each other much because we were both travelling. It is therefore pointless to constantly message each other, because there is no way we can meet until we are in the same place.

Finally, we were both back in London.

15 minutes before I finish working at an event, I give her the idea for a date to have that same day. I wanted to watch a movie, and it was a good opportunity to bring her along to it.

I throw in some humor to set the rhythm of not being a serious bastard.

She gets distracted a little from the main purpose of the conversation.

Let's get it back on track.

Time to figure out **logistics**.

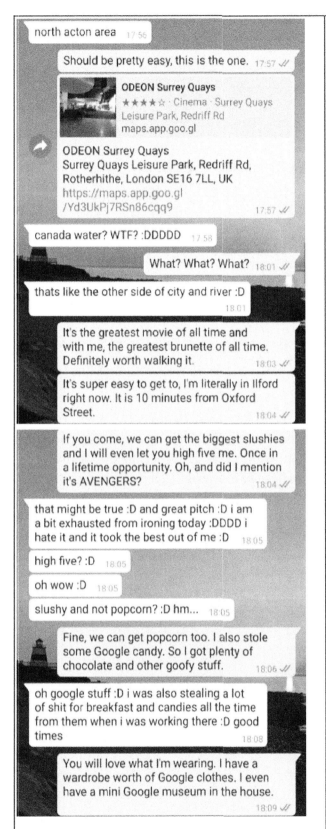

north acton area 17:56

Should be pretty easy, this is the one. 17:57

**ODEON Surrey Quays**
★★★★☆ · Cinema · Surrey Quays
Leisure Park, Rediff Rd
maps.app.goo.gl

ODEON Surrey Quays
Surrey Quays Leisure Park, Redriff Rd,
Rotherhithe, London SE16 7LL, UK
https://maps.app.goo.gl
/Yd3UkPj7RSn86cqq9 17:57

canada water? WTF? :DDDDD 17:58

What? What? What? 18:01

thats like the other side of city and river :D
18:01

It's the greatest movie of all time and
with me, the greatest brunette of all time.
Definitely worth walking it. 18:03

It's super easy to get to, I'm literally in Ilford
right now. It is 10 minutes from Oxford
Street. 18:04

If you come, we can get the biggest slushies
and I will even let you high five me. Once in
a lifetime opportunity. Oh, and did I mention
it's AVENGERS? 18:04

that might be true :D and great pitch :D i am
a bit exhausted from ironing today :DDDD i
hate it and it took the best out of me :D 18:05

high five? :D 18:05

oh wow :D 18:05

slushy and not popcorn? :D hm... 18:05

Fine, we can get popcorn too. I also stole
some Google candy. So I got plenty of
chocolate and other goofy stuff. 18:06

oh google stuff :D i was also stealing a lot
of shit for breakfast and candies all the time
from them when i was working there :D good
times 18:08

You will love what I'm wearing. I have a
wardrobe worth of Google clothes. I even
have a mini Google museum in the house.
18:09

I give her the details of the location.

It may be a little far away for her. But it's a very hyped movie and something she should not miss out on just because of an excuse. It is also near where I live, which gives me good **logistics.** One street away is as good as it gets.

Lots of emotions, possibly needs more convincing. But no more convincing needs to be done, so I assume it will happen.

Still a little off-topic.

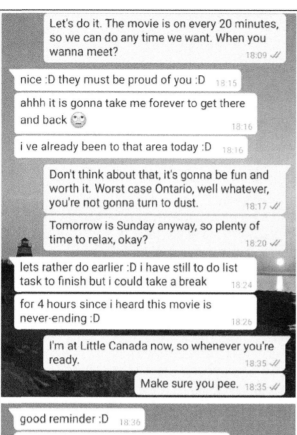

Back on track.

There is still a little resistance.

At this point, it is like being the voice inside her head that convinces her brain to do something she knows she wants to do.

She hasn't even confirmed yet, but I assume it is happening. This gives her the opportunity to, in her next message; tell me in some way if she is coming or not.

She is.

Now it's for real, this will happen.

Now she is focused on meeting.

Blah blah blah.

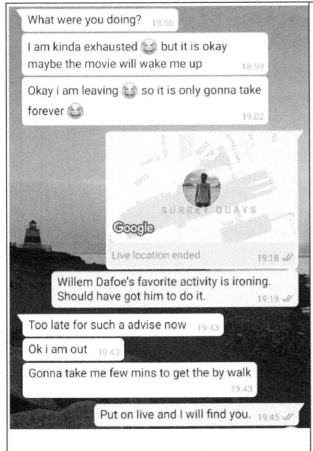

What were you doing? 18:56

I am kinda exhausted 😂 but it is okay maybe the movie will wake me up 18:59

Okay i am leaving 😂 so it is only gonna take forever 😂 19:02

Live location ended 19:18 ✓✓

Willem Dafoe's favorite activity is ironing. Should have got him to do it. 19:19 ✓✓

Too late for such a advise now 19:43

Ok i am out 19:43

Gonna take me few mins to get the by walk 19:43

Put on live and I will find you. 19:45 ✓✓

Now that she is leaving her place, I have a rough estimation of when she will arrive.

Gave her my location, she gave me hers. We found each other and had our date watching a movie. The movie screenings were all sold out for the next 2 hours, so we booked a later time and spent the waiting time eating at a place nearby. We then watched the movie and left the movie theater at 01:40 in the morning.

To summarize, it is important to push through and get to the point. Minimize distractions or things will become complicated; in other words, stay focused and loyal to the purpose of the conversation by pushing to meet and it will be more likely to happen.

**Today 23:49**

Let's skip all the bullshit. How adventurous are you?

How do you mean?

How good is your imagination? ; )
Can you name 3 things that would be amazing for a date?

1) go to a museum followed by drinks and food, 2) laying out in the sun chatting, drinking, having ice cream, 3) order pizza and watch Harry Potter or Lord of the Rings movies

People always forget about food when it comes to museums, you're on another level. I also just ate half of my ice cream watching Schitt's Creek. And maybe we can compromise on the pizza and make our own, I just got the ingredients and I really suck at it. Perfect, let's do it. Got WhatsApp?

Yeah I've got WhatsApp. My number is 074 **ICE ICE**

# Tinder

Sometimes clarity may be asked for, in which case it is better to turn it into getting her to imagine something for you.

This was casually done by asking which 3 things she would love to do for a date. The 3 things line.

She used her imagination to reveal what would potentially be the most perfect dates. Now you know what to do, and everything you need to know has been acquired in just 2 messages from her.

I reward her for her great response, and move it to WhatsApp.

# Choosing Words: What Should You Say?

Think to yourself... *'What should I say?'*

It does not entirely matter what you say, as long as what you say can be understood. Your communication needs to be as clear as possible. Not everyone is a native speaker of your language. If you are unsure of sending your message, before you send it to any girl, read it to yourself. Read it again, but in the voice of a nerd who doesn't know what a vagina looks like. If it makes sense in relation to that voice; if it sounds needy or desperate, it's probably not a message you should send. Now read it in a voice that is playful or masculine. Does it make sense? Does it work? Does it fit? Is this the kind of thing someone amazing or attractive would say? In order for a message to pass the most basic test, it needs to be a message that is not needy and that is not cringe-worthy. It also needs to achieve something. You cannot expect everyone to respond easily to a message that means nothing or a message that does not inspire the response of the other person. So it is important for you to think about how someone could possibly respond to what you are about to say.

There will also be cases where you may feel like the conversation has taken a turn where you do not necessarily want it to go. There is one word you can use to change the topic every single time. It is a very simple word: *'anyway.'* If the conversation goes off-topic or you need to push it in the right direction, use that word. *'Anyway'* lets you change one conversation about a particular thing into any conversation about any particular thing. It is very useful for getting back on track with your purpose of messaging her, which is to meet.

The recurring theme of the Message Game philosophy is that messaging must come with purpose, and that purpose is to meet. If you cannot meet someone because they are far away, there is really no point messaging them until it becomes easily possible to meet. For example, if you live in New York and you go to Hawaii for a week and have a holiday romance there with someone who was also visiting but lives in London, then quite clearly both of you live in completely different locations, and after that Hawaii experience both of you had to go separate ways. In that example, it will be a waste of time to be pen pals; you will certainly not be messaging each other for the rest of your lives. It's over, unless both of you meet again in another location. It is better to let the experience end on a high note than to let it drag on without purpose or practicality and just wither out and die.

Good communication must not be desperate or needy. It must be clear and it must go somewhere. Message game is not just words, you can use voice messages to communicate in more effective ways. Voice messages are beneficial provided that your voice is clear and confident, and not trembling or hesitant. It gives a more personal touch and gives a deeper sense of her knowing and exploring you. It is better to sense, in some ways, a picture of what is being communicated through voice messages. However, it is not for everyone.

There are generally three types of communication you should be aware of, and it defines everything.

1. Attraction
2. Comfort
3. Entertainment

Attraction communication is the attempt to build attraction. One notable example of attraction communication is sexting. This is not a focus of the Message Game philosophy because the whole point of being sexual is to have sex, and messaging about sex is not sex, and it is nowhere near as good as the act of having sex. Attraction communication is a minor part of Message Game philosophy because it should already be attractive enough in the fact that you are good at communicating and getting things done, such as meeting and working on your real interaction in the physical world.

Comfort communication is the attempt to build comfort. An example of comfort communication is if you are 25 years old and a woman aged 30 is hesitant about your age, it is then important to comfort her and communicate that the age difference is not a big deal and that you are comfortable with it as long as she is. Comfort communication is all about assuring her that something is not a problem. This is an important tool for shifting obstacles out of the way to solve any problems so that you can take steps forward.

Entertainment communication is the attempt to entertain. Most guys believe that entertaining a girl through messages is the key to getting a date or having sex. It's not. Messaging should not be to entertain each other without purpose. As a disclaimer, this is not to say that you should be boring when messaging people, this is to say that you should not be relying on trying to be funny. There is a huge misunderstanding in that so many people believe that entertaining her will be the way forward into meeting or building a relationship. If you are trying to entertain her and not trying to arrange to meet, you are wasting your time. If you are arranging to meet her and you are having fun in the process of messaging, that's great.

That last part really needs to be etched into your brain. You are arranging to meet her, and you are having fun. Having fun is secondary to arranging to meet. Arranging to meet is the whole purpose, and so you are not having fun and then arranging to meet, you are in fact messaging her in order to meet but communicating in positive ways. Priorities matter.

1. Think about how you may be perceived by her.
2. Think about her potential response.
3. You can change the direction of a conversation at any time you want.
4. Do not try to entertain her without trying to arrange to meet, you are not a clown.
5. Arrange to meet her.

**Tinder**

The first message aims at provoking a response to tell me if she is boring or not. Not many girls want to say they are boring, the point is that I get a response and possibly a little extra information.

She then responds to qualify herself to state that she is not boring, of course.

Then you can lead with a suggestion of an activity that you would like, or that her description suggests.

Confirm it.

Then get her phone number and arrange the time and place from there.

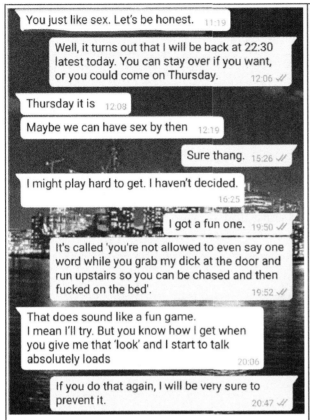

You just like sex. Let's be honest. 11:19

Well, it turns out that I will be back at 22:30 latest today. You can stay over if you want, or you could come on Thursday. 12:06

Thursday it is 12:08

Maybe we can have sex by then 12:19

Sure thang. 15:26

I might play hard to get. I haven't decided. 16:25

I got a fun one. 19:50

It's called 'you're not allowed to even say one word while you grab my dick at the door and run upstairs so you can be chased and then fucked on the bed'. 19:52

That does sound like a fun game. I mean I'll try. But you know how I get when you give me that 'look' and I start to talk absolutely loads 20:06

If you do that again, I will be very sure to prevent it. 20:47

## WhatsApp

Oh, no! She knows I want sex! What do I say next?!

Well, to start with, I didn't even acknowledge her comment. I simply jumped right into letting her know when I will be available.

I didn't even react to her second comment either, I am not messaging her to negotiate the terms and conditions of sex, or to argue my way into having sex, or to prove myself that I am worthy of sex. What matters is whether we will meet in the future.
Once we meet, anything can happen anyway.

I then came up with a fun turn-around for her third comment, and she was drawn into it.

And to remind you once again, originally she accused me of just wanting sex. After these messages, we still had sex.

Let's skip all the bullshit. How spontaneous are you?

Sun, Feb 19, 19:33

I like to think I'm pretty spontaneous

What's your idea of spontaneity?

I'm guessing that you're a fangirl for wine or something quite classy. If that's the case, I can crack open my vodka.

Mon, Feb 20, 12:19

That sounds good

I'm not as classy as my photos might suggest

I can be very un-classy

Mon, Feb 20, 19:54

Oh stop it. 😊

I'm not classy anyway. I'm a Marxist.

So what will the drinks be?

Mon, Feb 20, 21:17

Nice

Wheeeeeey

I am very flexible when it comes to that

Whiskey?

## Tinder

Line sent.

What do I say if she asks something back?

This conversation took three screenshots to cover. It involved some conversation about classiness and alcohol.

Sometimes you will get a response back asking for more detail about what you said. You cannot always prepare for when such things happen, but you can learn one simple thing.

It doesn't matter entirely what was said. On the next page you can see me ask if she has WhatsApp, I asked the question in two words. The trend you have seen so far has been that girls are very inclined into giving their phone numbers on Tinder pretty easily.

Mon, Feb 20, 22:22

Good choice for you, but I'm sticking to vodka unless you can intoxicate me to such a point that I cannot tell the difference.

Got WhatsApp?

b 21, 18:05

07

The first reason is that if you're doing this quick, you're not messing around. You're not trying really hard to impress anyone. But just imagine what her other messages are like, other guys are most likely trying to impress her or saying things that are going absolutely nowhere.

The second reason is that everything said here has a reason to it, and that reason is to get the job done. To meet. To actually serve as something that isn't pointless or that isn't 'just another conversation on the Internet'.

**Tinder**

Today 19:26

Let's skip all the bullshit. How adventurous are you?

Today 19:51

I'll give you some examples and I'll let you be the judge:
I've been to 50 countries, many of which I've solo backpacked, I've climbed a volcano, mountaineered up a glacier, visited Madagascar and Cameroon, I've tried flying trapeze, ...

She gave lots of examples to qualify herself in her answer to my opener. These are extremely adventurous, which means that she is a very fun person.

Today 20:41

Your bio is literally everything I am here for. I'm stunned. Let's fucking do some of it, got WhatsApp? I didn't know there was an Olympic Park slide.

I just got back to London this morning.

I then looked at the bio, confirmed that we should do one of the things mentioned in her bio that she wanted to do, and proceeded to WhatsApp.

Today 21:00

Damn! And totally, let's! My whatsapp is 07 **ICE ICE**

Passion.

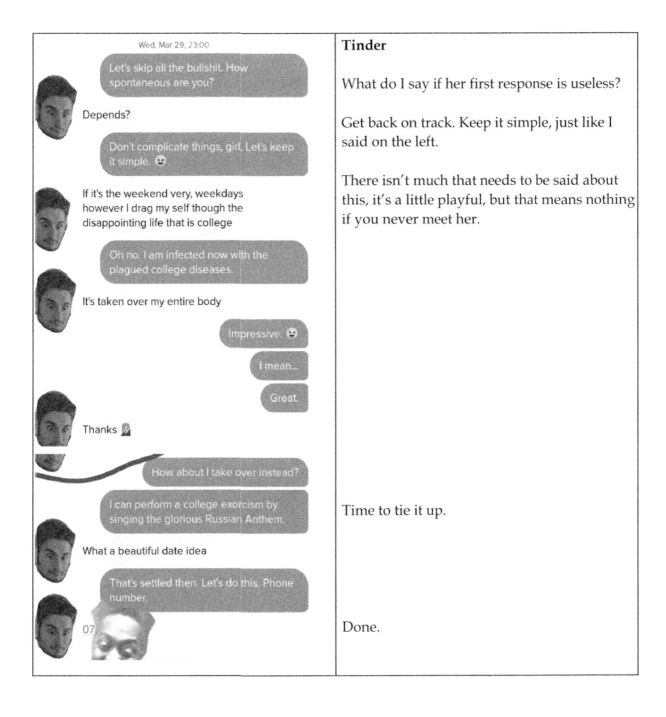

**Tinder**

What do I say if her first response is useless?

Get back on track. Keep it simple, just like I said on the left.

There isn't much that needs to be said about this, it's a little playful, but that means nothing if you never meet her.

Time to tie it up.

Done.

---

### Chat transcript (from image)

Wed, Mar 29, 23:00

Let's skip all the bullshit. How spontaneous are you?

Depends?

Don't complicate things, girl, Let's keep it simple. 😊

If it's the weekend very, weekdays however I drag my self though the disappointing life that is college

Oh no. I am infected now with the plagued college diseases.

It's taken over my entire body

Impressive. 😜

I mean...

Great.

Thanks 🙍

How about I take over instead?

I can perform a college exorcism by singing the glorious Russian Anthem.

What a beautiful date idea

That's settled then. Let's do this. Phone number.

07

When then. 16.43

TODAY

Tomorrow. 13:06

I'm not staying over. 13:08

If you insist. 13:13

Wash your sheets. 13:13

What time. 15:39

I will be back at 18:30, roughly. 15:56

I'll swing by after work
I actually can't stay though. Also we
genuinely can't have sex
16:04

Of course, I'm saving myself for marriage.
16:21

I mean we all know that's a lie 16:24

No sex. Just blowjobs 16:26

Good. My wife will accept that. 16:38

## WhatsApp

She is investing, I am replying in a very vague way.

She attempted to take sex off the table. Most guys will fall into the **shit test** trap here and react to it. The solution is not to react to it. So I jokingly said that I am saving myself for marriage. I'm obviously not. I am not a virgin. It's a joke. She knows that.

You need to learn that being serious throughout your 'conversations' is fucking boring. Loosen up, take risks and be playful.

She then said that, of course, it is a lie. She then puts oral sex on the table, but still declares that standard sex is off the table. I made another light comment, not reacting or playing into it, and we had sex later that day anyway.

The moral of the story is to never fall for it.

## Instagram

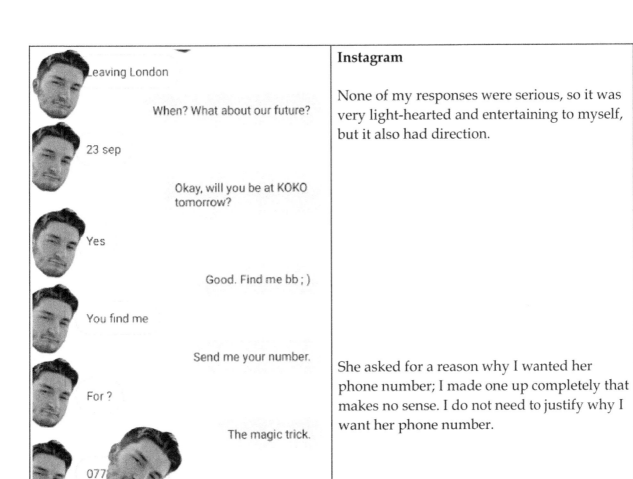

eaving London

> When? What about our future?

23 sep

> Okay, will you be at KOKO tomorrow?

Yes

> Good. Find me bb ; )

You find me

> Send me your number.

For ?

> The magic trick.

077

None of my responses were serious, so it was very light-hearted and entertaining to myself, but it also had direction.

She asked for a reason why I wanted her phone number; I made one up completely that makes no sense. I do not need to justify why I want her phone number.

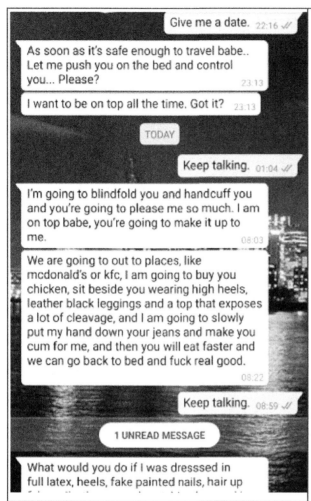

**WhatsApp**

She's very forward and invested, which means I can get her to give more with little effort.

Two words.

She gives me two paragraphs.

Two words.

It goes on.

Let's skip all the bullshit. How adventurous are you?

**ICE** I'm very but it'd like to be! What kind of adventures do you like?

Food, pillow fights, cooking, boats, anything fun really. What would go down well with you?

**ICE** All of the above

Having a pillow fight on a boat with food is pretty dangerous, I don't think it will end well! I will whack you off the boat and take all the food for myself. ; )

I'm really craving milkshakes and stuff, we could do that and a pillow fight/movie. Good idea? ; )

**ICE** Only if the milkshakes are dairy free
🌀 What are we watching?

Do dairy free milkshakes exist?

Whatever we want. Porn. Spiderman. Maybe a TV show. I really need some ideas on that one. My list is too long.

**ICE** I've never had one but there must be. Theres dairy free ice cream! Lol Porn?! Maybe Severn i know you a bit better. I want to see Spider-Man again though

So good.

Which Spiderman?

**Tinder**

Line sent.

Great start. Suggestions.

Agreement.

Arranging what to do.

Milkshakes may be a problem, but the movie is good.

Choose movie.

Spiderman.

Which Spiderman?

| | |
|---|---|
| Lool | Movie specified. |
| **ICE** The last one with Tom Holland | |
| Sunday 22:36 | |
| Okay, so that's 1x Spiderman movie and 20x cuddles, would you like anything else with that order, ma'am? | Order placed. |
| **ICE** A couple more cuddles and I'll be good | Confirmation made. |
| You got it. Do you have WhatsApp? | |
| **ICE** I do indeed. But first i want to know what you're looking for on here? Aside from all the adventure of course | But wait… She knows it is too fast and wants to know what exactly I am looking for. She specified on her profile that she is looking for a relationship. |
| I'm just looking for something that feels good and special. | |
| **ICE** Hmmmm. Ok add me. 07 **ICE ICE** | |
| | Done. |

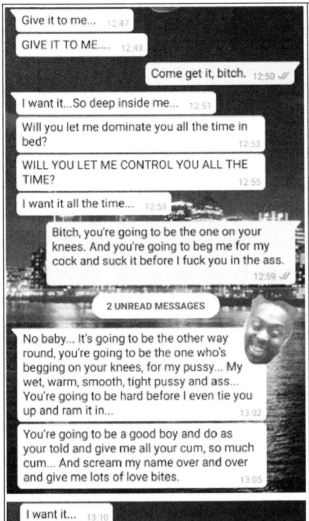

## WhatsApp

She's being sexual. I'm being straight to the point.

She is very desperate. This girl used to see me and at this point she hadn't seen me for a very long time. She remained extremely obsessed with me.

Explicit content. Parental guidance advised.

She's making it her life's mission.

She has been writing for 10 minutes now.

She's still really desperate.

Come get it. 13:15

She sent a picture of her boobs, but I edited my face onto it for the purpose of not showing you nudes in this book.

She went to go get it.

Today 17:16

Hi

You look like you have exciting life

**ICE** Tell me more about yourself

Today 18:02

Got WhatsApp? I may prefer to show some photos.

Today 18:18

**ICE** 07 **ICE ICE**

**Tinder**

She wants to know more.

Let's move it to WhatsApp, I already know she is interested.

Saturday 22:07

Let's skip all the bullshit. How adventurous are you?

**ICE** I'll do anything for you daddy

Good. Give me your WhatsApp.

**ICE** I'd prefer to keep it on here for now, is that ok with you? I'll tell you anything you want to know

Before we get to that, I would just like to take a moment to appreciate our mutual love for cats.

**ICE** Cats are brilliant right? The best animal on the planet

What if I told you...? I have 8 at home.

**ICE** Perfect

**ICE** Sometimes I like to dress up as one...

I would probably have to pet you and let you trap me in my bed.

**ICE** As long as I can scratch

And just look at you and think that my life can wait, this cat is too adorable to disturb.

**ICE** I'll purr just for you

I will give treats just for you and let you play with my laser pointer any time.

**ICE** Will you stroke me in return?

Always.

I will not go

**Tinder**

Her first response was amazing, but I did not want to fall into the trap of escalating the conversation in a sexual way; that's not what I am here for and I got bored of that years ago.

So instead, since she will 'do anything', I tell her to give me her phone number. She doesn't give it straight away, but that's okay. I can come back to that later.

In her bio, she mentioned loving cats. I decided to go on that, since nobody can out-cat me and my love of cats. This is a mutual interest that is powerful when both of you absolutely love the same thing. So I lead based on that.

She then says she likes to dress up, which is pretty sexy. But I purposefully avoiding making the conversation sexually obvious and proceed to almost troll her, but in a playful way just to see what happens.

It just goes on and on, really.

Unfortunately her profile was probably deleted or unmatched, but this would have been great if the phone number was received. Once a Tinder profile disappears, you will most likely never find that person again.

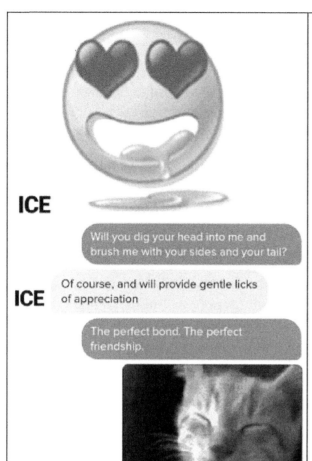

Such a shame. But this is why we take phone numbers fast in the first place.

# Other People's Messages: What Can You Learn?

Ask yourself: *'What can I learn?'*

What can you take from this? This is a special chapter that breaks down the messages of other people, instead of my own. This is important because if only my messages were shown, then the context and perspective would be very limited. By showing the messages of others, you can see different styles. Everyone is different. And of course, you can try to spot the mistakes yourself, but even more important than all this is the fact that you may have sent messages similar to those you are about to see. This will provide you with future references in order to improve.

Not all messages here are right or wrong; there is a mixture of positive and negative attempts at messaging. Not only will you be able to see what went wrong, but also you will identify what has been done right. You should also look out for messaging styles that you feel would be appropriate for your personality or your style, so let this chapter serve as a larger source of inspiration for your own potential. Any of these conversations could have happened to you.

All of these messages were collected from members of the Message Game group over the course of a few weeks. It is therefore quite necessary for me to declare that obviously, these are not full conversations, and some are just screenshots of just a few messages. This is because many members get excited when something happens and show us the messages before the next steps happen. But this is no problem. It will be very apparent as to which stage people are at and where the interaction can go from there.

Let's dive in and see what lessons we can learn from other guys.

**Someone's Messages**

Straight to the point is great.

Although she loves that it does not waste time, she just needs comfort in knowing whether or not this guy is worth her time. So in this case, don't be sending lots of messages after receiving one like this. You can simply just say that it may be worth the risk or that the whole point is to meet.

13 hours ago

Heya Hun 😎 let's skip the small talk are you free in the weekend ?

🔒 Unlock Read Receipt

2 hours ago

You don't waste any time

2 hours ago

I like to know if it's worth meeting lol

## Someone's Messages

This person started a conversation based on something written in her bio. He gives a 'push' and then gets straight to the point.

She likes that it is straight to the point. To girls, it is often a breath of fresh air. At the same time, she doesn't want to give herself away too easily by declaring that he will have to work for it.

He responded in almost exactly the same manner, which does not exactly solve the problem or move it forward to receiving her phone number, so i t can be taken as a step back. Instead of acting like a sassy fat princess, he could have focused on ignoring her last message and proceeding to finding a reasonably easy way to obtain her phone number by providing comfort to her hesitation of giving the phone number.

Wednesday 01:00

Lol unmatch me

I will definately not prove that 😄

Wednesday 18:55

Your wish is my command beautiful X

Wednesday 21:38

Then give me your number.

Wednesday 22:19

Straight to the point - I like it

But I'm a tease so you'll have to work for it otherwise bye X

Today 01:19

Well i'm a catch so you're gonna have to impress me otherwise bye.

Sent

## Someone's Messages

This person poked a t the girl that she is becoming a little out of touch. She did not exactly take it that well, but at least it spills the beans that she liked having her bean flicked.

The mere fact that she wrote a lot in her own defense goes to show that she cares about how she is viewed by this guy.

won't hangout with you. You seem to be depressed or something too negative you used to be more fun! ☺

Really? What makes you think that? How can you tell how fun I am? You never take me out anywhere. You usually show up at my place at 3:00 a.m. or even later sometimes (after a night out at a bar). We have good sex and then you leave the next day because you have other things to do. I haven't seen you in four months. How the hell can you tell whether I am depressed or not as fun? I am  curious. Please tell me.

I am still waiting for a response to this text.

 Indulge me. Seriously.

**Someone's Messages**

This was actually made famous as a meme. Her name is Sophie and the guy is trying to use clever ways of becoming sexual through messages.

But that's not important. The important part is that so many guys think that in acting this way - by trying to entertain girls or trying to be clever in the messaging maze in every conversation will get them results. It won't. You will just be wasting mental energy and going nowhere. Don't try to be clever like this.
Yes, it's funny. But not every girl is called Sophie, and if you try to have clever responses to girls, you will have to be able to think quickly for every possible message you receive.

I think your name is missing an n
Mon 12:37

Becuase you Sophine you blow my mind
Mon 12:38

That made my day
13:30

I can make your tomorrow too
Now

I can also make your hole weak
Now

## Someone's Messages

A follower of my Message Game techniques used a very similar approach, solidifying both the phone number and the date at the same time.

He is very focused on the objective and therefore more likely to complete it.

Wed, 6 Feb, 07:27

Let's cut all the bullshit. How spontaneous are you?

Wed, 6 Feb, 11:27

 It depends! On how much risk is involved

Wed, 6 Feb, 14:21

Fair enough. Let's say a cute stranger asks you out for drinks to get to know you. Would you be down for that?

Wed, 6 Feb, 16:32

 Sounds like a worthwhile risk! I'm free tomorrow and Friday for a drink

Wed, 6 Feb, 17:11

Let's do tomorrow night then

Got Whatsapp?

Wed, 6 Feb, 17:33

 Sounds good. My WhatsApp number is +140

## Someone's Messages

What a mess. It's a bad attempt.

First of all, it uses plurality. It is not about oneself, it includes everyone of that description so she can quite easily pick someone else. Second of all, there just isn't much to it.

Ok how do you feel about drinks with cute boys?

Sent

Monday 22:15

 Oh then I come up with an answer: please wait in line

**Someone's Messages**

One of those 'depending girls'.

When this guy posted this in the Message Game group, everyone loved it because she took it straight to sex.

> Lets skip all the small talk how spontaneous are you?

Depends on the activity sweetcheeks

> Giving you a full body massage
>
> Sent

Full body massage wants to be short for dick if its expecting anyone to be spontaneous in this weather

---

**Someone's Messages**

Not a good start. As for the second line, a comedian would not say they are funny, just like a tall person wouldn't say they are tall, just like a weightlifter wouldn't say they are strong. It should be very apparent without needing to declare it. Here's a better one. It's like a black guy saying he's black.

Now for the third line... He says that the chat was fun. A girl would think he has probably never had a fun conversation before. He was ignored, and that is no surprise to me.

He tried again the next day. And hours later, still reacted to her story. And replied again.

This behavior is too needy and the guy is trying to qualify himself too much; making his value a lot lower than hers.

Sat 4:06 AM

Hey bad girl

Ryan here the funny guy from Singapore

Fun chatting with u at circus club

Cirque le soir*

Sun 1:44 PM

Wanna grab a coffee and drink next week?

Sun 9:55 PM

You reacted to their story

You replied to their story

## Someone's Messages

Yes, lady. This is exactly why I made this opener. She appreciates that it comes from getting shit done instead of asking stupid common questions or sending messages that lead nowhere.

The obstacle, however, is the last thing she said, but it can easily be eradicated simply by declaring that the point of the adventure is to get to know each other.

Messages are not f or exchanging life stories or getting to know each other. Dates are for that, or alcoholics anonymous meetings.

> Let's skip all the bullshit. How spontaneous are you?

vendredi 17:06

THANKS GOD ! Finally someone who don't want to know if I'm fine cause obviously everybody answer yes to that stupid question..
Hm, i can give u an example of my spontaneity : one day after an exam i was really stressed cuz my last exam was the newt day and I needed to destress so I decided to take my car an just drive without knowing were, so I drove for like 3 hours and I felt so good but a little bit stressed .. so I quit the highway and I was in arles and i saw a place were they proposed bungee jumping.. and i just decided to jump .. I've never been so fucking relaxed for my entiere life.. and after I decided to go see the sea and returned in Toulouse so peacefull and destressed !

What's the most incredible thing you did during your short life?

Aujourd'hui 15:03

> Well, it must have been that time when I skipped the bullshit and took Inès on an adventure! Got WhatsApp?

Aujourd'hui 15:26

Lets see if u r the personn i think u r before i give u my whatsapp okay?

**Someone's Messages**

Some phrases used here were directly copied from the Choosing Words chapter, but added a slight twist in inspiration.

She's open to it, perfect. Now it is time for him to arrange the time and place. Nothing more.

Dec 30, 2017 4:49 am

Let's cut to the chase, how spontaneous are you?

Yesterday - 2:00 pm

hm well what kinda spontaneous we talking about?

Today - 5:42 pm

I'm guessing you're a fangirl for wine or something quite classy. If that's the case, I can crack open my vodka.

well vodka sounds good to me :p

## Someone's Messages

This is what I call a 'defining girl'. She wants more detail to picture what this is about. She cooperates quite well, so now it is time to arrange something.

Lets skip all the small talk. How spontaneous are you?

Today 19:22

Definition of spontaneous?

Adventurous

I can work with that

Tell me 3 things you want to do on our first date

Sent

Today 22:12

Hmmmm

Have a drink

Somewhere adventurous

& you can chose the last one xo

**Someone's Messages**

Quick and easy. She cannot do it on that day, but she says that the weekend is good. Perfect. Proceed to the arrangements.

Adventurous, easy going, and savage. Life of the party! Loving life and

In response:
Let's skip all the bullshit. How spontaneous are you?

What do you have in mind

Today - 3:51 PM

Having a nice dinner and after that we see

Sure I can't tonight though. This weekend ?

**Someone's Messages**

This is what I call an 'out of 10 girl'.

She gives details of her timings.

The conversation proceeded to arrange for the same day. Very well played.

> Let's cut to the chase, how spontaneous are you?

Today 13:07

Pretty spontaneous... Out of 10 I would rate it a solid 8...

> Perfect 😈 what's your availability like today?

Work till 6 then no plans...m

What's your idea lmao x

> I'm thinking drinks at 8 and then we'll see from there

Drinks at 8 sound perfect... The we will see from there can hold off for now lmao ;)

| | |
|---|---|
| Location given.<br><br>Looks like a great interaction so far, it's a very solid arrangement.<br><br><br><br><br><br>He did it. | **Sounds great to me! Revolution or** ▬▬▬<br><br>Perfect 😊 shall meet you there sir! What's your first name? Xx<br><br>▬▬ **actually is my first name** 🫠 **little odd. See you soon!**<br>Sent<br><br>It's not odd lol. It's different but it's quite nice actually! Shall see you later :) x |
| **Someone's Messages**<br><br>It was inevitable. | Feb 2 6:13 pm<br><br>**Let's cut to the chase, how spontaneous are you?**<br><br>Today - 10:27 pm<br><br>I'm spontaneous<br><br>You like eating pussy?<br><br>**Yes I do. Do you like deep throats baby?**<br><br>Yeahh<br><br>**I like it. Got WhatsApp?**<br><br>Just now!<br><br>0▬▬▬ |

**Someone's Messages**

On a serious note, don't try this on everyone. But it will inevitably work on certain types of girls. I tried it myself once just to see how funny it would be. I got unmatched. But this guy pulled it off.

Today 16:46

> Let's skip the bullshit , how spontaneous are you ?

I'd say very spontaneous hahaha u?

> Would you let me lick Nutella off the booty ?

Booty, tits, legs 😊

---

**Someone's Messages**

I actually have no idea what happened here. It hurts just to read it, but she actually asked him for his number.

YOU MATCHED WIT█████ ██ 12/03/2018.

> Lets skip all the bullshit, how spontaneous are you?

the way you look. i dont think you should be complaining about anything.

> Yeah it keeps me up late, i spend my days crying over how i look

> Are you ok?

depends

> Have guys hurt you a lot in the past or are your parents divorced? - feel free not to answer if its uncomfortable

ok, whtz ur nuum?

| | |
|---|---|
| **Someone's Messages**<br><br>Ooh, interesting. Smooth. | LIKE A COSMOS FLOWER......ViBer me for more details<br><br>In response:<br>Let's skip all the bullshit. How spontaneous are you?<br><br>Today - 1:15 PM<br><br>Enough to runaway with you 😜 😅<br><br>Today - 3:50 PM<br><br>Let's run away to my room<br><br>Today - 4:06 PM<br><br>lets go!!<br><br>WhatsApp? |
| **Someone's Messages**<br><br>Perfect, I guess. | Lets skip all the small talk. How spontaneous are you?<br><br>Στάλθηκε<br><br>I'm really horny if that's what u mean and I wouldn't mind being fucked rn |

## Someone's Messages

Her response proves that she believes in the philosophy of Message Game - to meet.

She is also available f or the entire day, so they both pursued to meet in short notice.

> Relatively reserved and quiet type of person who believes truth should be more important than peoples sensitivities

> In response:
> Let's skip all the bullshit. How spontaneous are you?

Today - 12:34 PM

Meet me and you'll know

What's your time schedule today?

Today - 1:06 PM

I'm free today anytime

Where

Today - 5:09 PM

Malate

I stay in red planet

Red like your cold blood hehe

Today - 6:52 PM

Lol so you want me to come over?

Just now!

Nie?

Now?

## Someone's Messages

The way she messages is like she has a lot of energy and curiosity. Five exclamation points in the first response.

Three questions in the second response.

Five individual lines of messages in the third response. It was funny.

Let's cut the small talk, how spontaneous are you?

Thursday 20:57

Okay!!!! I feel like I need to be more spontaneous!

Yesterday 14:08

I like it, where are you from?

Yesterday 19:23

Are you spontaneous?
I'm from Northamptonshire near Daventry? How about yourself?

Yesterday 20:30

Coventry

Do you have WhatsApp?

Sent

I do indeed lovely

077

Hit me up bitch

Sorry

That was aggressive

**Someone's Messages**

Basic girl.

He asks for her favorite drink, she doesn't cooperate. Then she does. The moral of the story is to not give up just because of one small response.

None of those

But know alot of people from all three categories

Monday 8:12 PM

Hahaha...basic gurl 😜

What's your favorite drink

😆 😆 thanks but no thanks

Monday 10:13 PM

It's a quiz

so we won't be going for drinks on our date anymore...

Monday 11:12 PM

Lol, I drink spirits and whiskey

**Someone's Messages**

It could happen. In such a situation, move to WhatsApp ASAP.

Let's skip the small talk, how spontaneous are you?

Sent

Show me dick

## Someone's Messages

He asked for how spontaneous she is. She doesn't quite get it, so he reframed to pizza. She really doesn't get it, she seems pretty dumb. So he reframed it again to meeting instead of chatting, which was a great way of communicating it and got straight to the point instead of explaining things to her like she is a dumb 5 year old.

Hey let's skip all the bullshit. How spontaneous are you?

Gestern 18:05

Spontaneous for what?

A pizza 🍕 yum

Sorry. I don't get ur point

Gestern 20:53

I wanna meet you baby instead of chatting

Chatting is so boring

Gesendet

Gestern 21:56

Yeah. Why not

## Someone's Messages

Straight to the point, once again. Works out really well. She loves it.

> Hey let's skip all the bullshit. How spontaneous are you?

Gestern 20:36

Hey

What bullshit are you talking about?

Sorry I just replied  I was working today

> You know ... all that chit chat

> Let's just meet

Haha

Tomorrow after work maybe?

Where are you staying?

Now I'm so sleepy babe

**Someone's Messages**

Nicely done. She put up a barrier of not wanting to go to his p lace because she doesn't really know him. But that's not a problem, just a little bit of comfort is needed. His fun personality conveyed through the messages helps comfort her with the idea of meeting for pizza at his place.

Hey let's skip all the bullshit. How spontaneous are you?

Gestern 14:40

Hahahahaag

Very spotaneous.

Gestern 16:43

Cool

Let's eat some pizza in my place

And have fun

Gestern 17:20

Sorry i dont usually go to a strangers place.

Gestern 18:08

Do i look so strange? 💀

Gesendet

Gestern 20:43

Hahaha not so

| | |
|---|---|
| **Someone's Messages**<br><br>She specifies 'anything but sex', but this doesn't mean they won't have sex.<br><br>The German speakers of Message Game are doing very well. | Hey let's skip all the bullshit. How spontaneous are you?<br><br>Gestern 13:43<br><br>Super spontaneous<br><br>Im down whatever u have in your mind except sex<br><br>Gestern 16:44<br><br>What about a hug? 💀<br>Gesendet<br><br>Yes that will do |
| **Someone's Messages**<br><br>It all happened so fast. | Lets skip the bs. How spontaneous are you?<br><br>Spontaneous to go out tomorrow but not tonight<br><br>Perfect. Let's get out here. What's your #<br>Sent<br><br> |

**Someone's Messages**

One of our London-based followers using the Message Game mindset and putting it to practical use.

Hahaha haha

Where are you

Lol

Come meet me

Where?

Where are you ?

Xoyo

XOYO is a club in East London.

Oh shit I like that club

Really?!

Yea

Oh wow

I'm so drunk

His responses are very basic and short, he just needs to get to the point now.

You should have invited me

You were not replying mate

Hahaha lul I was sleeping

I am going out myself now

And you are posting photos and videos with socmant girls

She is jealous, but she loves it.

The power of Instagram allowed him to share the social proof of himself having fun with different girls. She noticed that and specifically admitted that she noticed how 'pretty and skinny' they are. This means that she sees that this guy has value.

So many

And they are so pretty and skinny lol

What about them ?

Do you wanna be on it ?

They are better than. Me

Awww don't sell your self short babe

She is now comparing herself to other girls.

Im serious

You're handsome

You can every girl

And you're so confront

Confident

She is pouring her heart out here.

My role model hahahha

**Someone's Messages**

It's a spontaneity contest.

WhatsApp or Instagram?

Alternatively, Snapchat?

Competing with each other.

> Lets skip all the small talk. How spontaneous are you?

Today 20:11

An unrealistically amount of spontaneous 🧑

So we don't waste my time. How spontaneous are you?

> I am definitely more spontaneous than you

Today 21:24

I highly doubt that

It really don't get more spontaneous than me

> I don't believe that cause i know for a fact i more spontaneous

> Do you have whatsapp or insta?

Oxi

And yes

Which one do you want

Have you got snap ?

> Haha ti oxi?ime siouros

> Yeah whats your snap

Today 21:49

> Let me prove you that i am more spontaneous than you

| | |
|---|---|
| Snapchat ID given. A little messy, but try not to give too many options when closing. WhatsApp will be good enough. | Today 22:47<br><br>Den ise siouros. You think you're correct 😂<br><br><br><br>We'll progress onto WhatsApp and insta after you show me how spontaneous you can be 😄 |
| **Someone's Messages**<br><br>Asking when she is free is one of the most important questions you could ever ask. It's all about meeting.<br><br><br><br><br><br>Knowing the activity is also important. | When are you free?<br><br>Or Sunday but evening about 8 pm ?<br><br>Sounds good but what time do you work the next day?<br><br>7<br><br>Ohhh, so i am not gonna see you for a long time<br><br>So what do you wanna do? Go out for food?<br><br>Or you can cook for me xd<br><br>Yeah thats better :D |

**Someone's Messages**

Something about a workout.

4 March 2019, she declares that she is busy for the whole week; this day was a Monday.

He replied the next d ay, on Tuesday. Not a good idea. This left his message as 'read' because the conversation for the rest of the week is simply pointless; she is busy.

What he should have done is not open or respond to her message until later that week, so that she could reply on, for example, Sunday when she is able to see her availabilities for the following week more clearly.

Hope you enjoyed your first Oslo 😄 my knees are slightly pissed at me for those deep squats 15:11 ✓✓

I did! Hahaha it was a good workout. 18:07

Yes I would recommend we arrange some follow up sessions :P 19:59 ✓✓

Haha glad you liked it. My roommate and I will be going out again soon to Oslo. 21:23

4 MARCH 2019

Haha cool was actually thinking we go for a matcha or other caffeinared beverage :) 14:22 ✓✓

That sounds nice too - I have family and friends over this week and weekend. So perhaps sometime after that? 23:24

5 MARCH 2019

Yes am a little busy till then anyways so that sounds good 16:49 ✓✓

**Someone's Messages**

I'm a little freaked out.

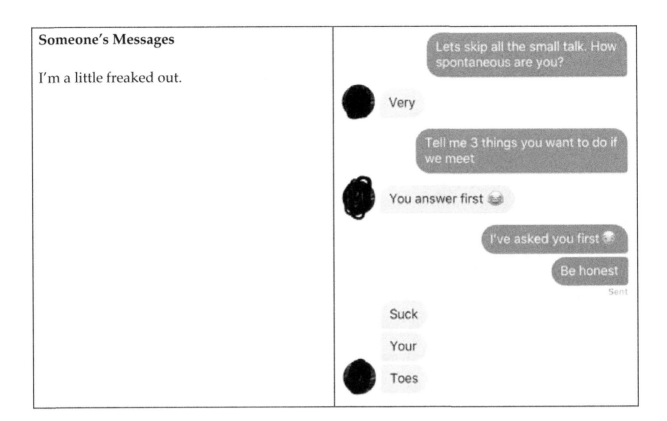

## Someone's Messages

This guy literally copy-and-pasted most of the lines from one example in this book with absolutely no context and it still worked.

That example is on page 161.

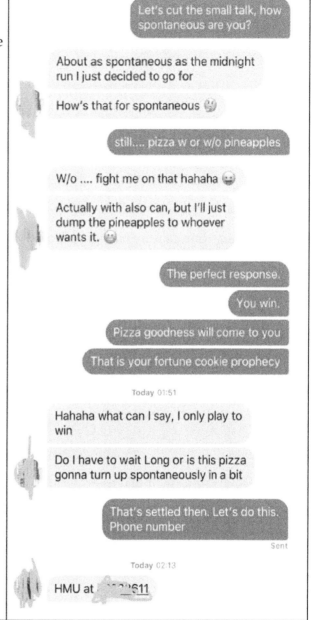

| **Someone's Messages** | Lets skip all the small talk. How spontaneous are you? |
| --- | --- |
| The word 'depends' is quite common in receiving a response to the classic spontaneous line. | All depends on the mood I'm in |
| | I can be extremely ready or be a potato |
| | That's the spectrum we're working with here |
| | Same |
| The new 3 things line captures imagination more. | Tell me 3 things you want to do if we meet |
| | Sent |
| | Well, if I had complete control of what we did I say we eat burgers go to a comedy show and get drinks after |
| | That sounds like quite the fun time for me |
| She has good communication, so she is more likely to be a really good person to date. | Mostly Cus I wanna see if you smile |
| | Your pictures are so serious  |
| | But how about you? |

## Someone's Messages

The first message h ere refers to her bio on Tinder. Her response is playful.

It's even more playful.

Now for the real stuff. It's important to get things done instead of attempt to flirt or be playful forever.

Goes off-topic a little once again.

Time to get back on topic.

Time to number-close.

I never thought it possible to find someone else who loves avocado as much as I... but alas love has no boundaries

That's funny because I also share your enthusiasm for garlic bread

Yesterday 23:53

Play your cards right and there could be a garlic bread themed wedding incoming

That's funny

Lets skip the boring stuff.. how adventurus are you Sophie ?

P.s as a PT i will be expecting you to squat me

Unfortunately as a PT with a knee injury squatting u is not currently an option

A piggy back will suffice

Haha then a piggy back it is

Tell me 3 things we's get up to if we hung out. I'll give you some clues: pillow fights, G-bread baking competition, and lazer tag

We would get up to*

We've definitely got to have an avocado rose making competition too

That sounds wild, you have good enthusiam.. got Whatsapp?

Haha yeah 0

See you on the other side

117

| Someone's Messages | |
|---|---|
| | Howdy! It's Chris from the thing |
| Chris from Texas showed me this. | Hi Chris!!! From the thing. You are so funny lol 😅 |
| | You are a cutie! |
| | Why don't you have plans on this Friday evening? |
| | It's only 8pm and thank you 😊 |
| | how spontaneous are you compared to the average girl? |
| A version of the spontaneous line. | It just depends. I'm kinda a spur of the moment at times s what about you? |
| She asks quite a lot of questions, but they are mainly aimed at meeting. This is a good sign and a big IOI. | Big plans this evening? |
| | Always... how spontaneous do you feel tonight? |
| Yes, Chris. Now we're talking. | Kinda of, what do you have in mind? |
| | Lol 😄 |
| | Spontaneous bumble date on a Friday night. I'm breaking all the dating rules 😎 |
| Emotional spike. | What. What!!! |
| | Flirty fun conversation over drinks at a local bar. You game? |
| He asks if she is up f or it or not. | Sure! Where? |
| | What part of town are you located? |
| She wants to do this. Now for **logistics**. | Uptown/downtown...near love field airport? You? |

They have now told each other their locations.

He gives the place to meet at.

He left her place the next morning. They did naughty things together.

I work in north west Dallas. Let me look up a good bar to meet up

Are you still at work?

About to leave... let's do inwood tavern, sounds good?

**Inwood Tavern**
goo.gl

Inwood Tavern
4119, 7717 Inwood Rd, Dallas, TX 75209
(214) 353-2666

Inwood tavern at 9:30pm... 👍 or 👎?

Sure!!!!

I'll see you there.

**Someone's Messages**

That's a deal.

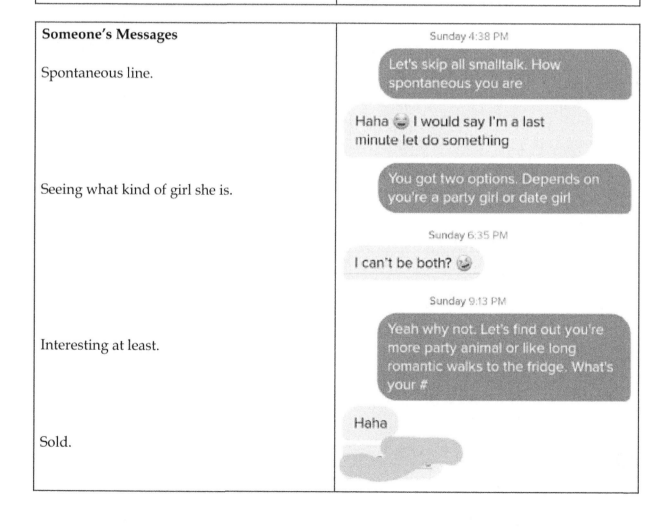

Lets skip all the small talk. How spontaneous are you?

Today 08:31

Very, how about you

Today 12:23

A lot

Tell me 3 things you want to do if we meet

Sent

Have good company, have good food, have good sex

---

**Someone's Messages**

Spontaneous line.

Seeing what kind of girl she is.

Interesting at least.

Sold.

Sunday 4:38 PM

Let's skip all smalltalk. How spontaneous you are

Haha 😄 I would say I'm a last minute let do something

You got two options. Depends on you're a party girl or date girl

Sunday 6:35 PM

I can't be both? 😜

Sunday 9:13 PM

Yeah why not. Let's find out you're more party animal or like long romantic walks to the fridge. What's your #

Haha

## Someone's Messages

We received these screenshots as it was happening. We were very interested in what was going to happen next.

She is being sassy with the accusation of this guy copying and pasting the opener. Did he copy and paste? Yes. At least he sent a message. What right does she have to complain when she was not the one to send the first message?

She proceeded to rant a little. Nobody really fucking cares, lady. Immediately after she sent these last messages, she unmatched him. If she is so quick to judge and cast someone potentially amazing out of her life, then she made a big mistake and it is her loss. She will drown in her own dating frustrations.

Needless to say, if you're the woman who wrote this and you're reading this, so many female profiles do not even have a bio. You lost a good man and that's your problem. You're not going to get far.

Today 5:55 PM

Let's cut to the chase, how spontaneous are you?

Presumably more than you are if you're copy/pasting the same intro line to every match.

Today 6:50 PM

Haha so I guess you're not that spontaneous...

Today 7:14 PM

I mean, if I was, I assume you'd just drop into the next line of your bit, here

Next time you could try this neat thing called reading? It's where you actually check somebody's profile out before sending a copy/paste message trying to play the numbers game. It comes across a lot more genuine.

**Someone's Messages**

Our school of thought that is discussed in the Message Game group brings some new insights on a regular basis. In February 2019, we discussed re-engaging old conversations with random Umbrella Academy GIFs; my idea. It worked on some, of course, which brings to wonder why they didn't respond in the first place, but none of that matters; you cannot do anything about it other than send a GIF and hope for the b est.

This was the first attempt made by someone to achieve the same result. This guy also mixed in March 2019's new idea, also by myself, to bring about three date ideas.

Look what happened, and this was found quite common when we first started rolling out the idea.

Perfect.

Fri, Feb 22, 6:22 PM

Let's cut to the chase, how spontaneous are you?

Thursday 8:52 PM

Today 9:58 PM

Shit! Well I definitely deleted the app at the wrong time!

Today 10:40 PM

Name me 3 things u'd wanna do if we met up

Do you want the tame and sweet or the fun and exciting answer?

Go for all.

Tame and sweet! I'd want to go to a farmers market, choose a picnic with each other, and sit in the park to just talk and enjoy a sunny afternoon

Fun and exciting! Slap my ass, pull my hair, and make me scream your name!

**Someone's Messages**

+10 points for Spiderman 3 GIFs.

Ice's adventurous line.

Beautiful idea.

No more needs to be said, so it's time to get the number.

She likes the quick moves. It is important to get things done quickly, otherwise it will be more likely to remain unfinished.

Youre cute..

How adventurous are you Chlo

I'd say quite! Why so ♥

Hope you are up for pizza eating compeitions and naked pillow fights

Oh I definitely am

We've found a winner

Whats your number, we are moving to Whatsapp

You move quick! I like that

Stop it youre making me blush Chlo

See you on the other side

Sent

| Someone's Messages | |
|---|---|
| | *Aujourd'hui 21:52* |
| Spontaneous line. | Let's cut the bullshit part, how spontaneous are you? |
| | *Aujourd'hui 22:17* |
| She's fucking agreeing. | Fucking spontaneous |
| | *Aujourd'hui 23:24* |
| Another reason why you shouldn't reply too quickly. | Are you good at sex |
| | Come and see |
| | But it will not happen tonight, I am on my period |
| Joking is good, it provides humor and stops her from seeing that he is taking up the offer too quickly. He therefore isn't desperate. | hahahaha |
| | You serious |
| | Tell me 3 things when we will meet, go |
| The 3 things line, created in 2019. | After you |
| | Foreplay, sex, abortion |
| Better not to argue, well played. | My turn |
| | Foreplay, sex, vanish |
| Perfect for some. | Got whatsapp? |

**Someone's Messages**

She opens.

This guy responded with the idea of a staring contest, which I gave in the Message Game group when he was wondering what to reply.

I left him with the task of coming up with something the loser has to do. He did well.

Too good to be true, ma'am? I know.

Maybe some more details, but not entirely necessary.

I know I'm about to sound really weird but you have intense eyes 😅

Yesterday 17:20

Your third photo tells me that you're the right candidate for a staring competition.

The loser has to declare her/his love for the other. Loud. In public.

I have a funny feeling you've done this before and won 🤨

But I'm down 👀

What public place makes you feel comfortable for declaring your love in front of random people?

I'm black belt in ninja staring martial arts.

I hope you don't mind 😎

Yesterday 18:54

In the middle of Las Vegas would be perfect, don't you think?

She is quite invested in the conversation and idea already.

> **Well I've lost already, damn it I knew I shouldn't have agreed to this!**

>> What happens in Vegas, stays in Vegas, and you love secrets. Good plan!

>> Let's discuss the details on Wzp

Yesterday 23:39

Time to move to WhatsApp.

> **Does wzp mean WhatsApp?**

> **How do you know I like sexrets?**

It's better to be very clear when you talk about something, it saves time.

>> Yes, we are moving to WhatsApp to continue the adventure .. what is your number

Sent

Well communicated. Done.

> **Okay sir 07~~~~**

**Someone's Messages**

This guy used the spontaneous line.

Absolutely no bullshit. Straight to the number close.

She gave him her phone number. All it took this guy was 2 messages to get it.

Yesterday, 3:45 PM

Hey Rosie, let's skip all the bullshit. How spontaneous are you?

id say a strong 6.5/10

Perfecto! Got WhatsApp?

0783

I will text you soon

Sent

## Someone's Messages

This is in fact the same guy and the same girl from the previous page. He is now contacting her by using her phone number.

Some bullshit about names.

This is where she was about to stop responding. This guy asked the group why she would stop here.

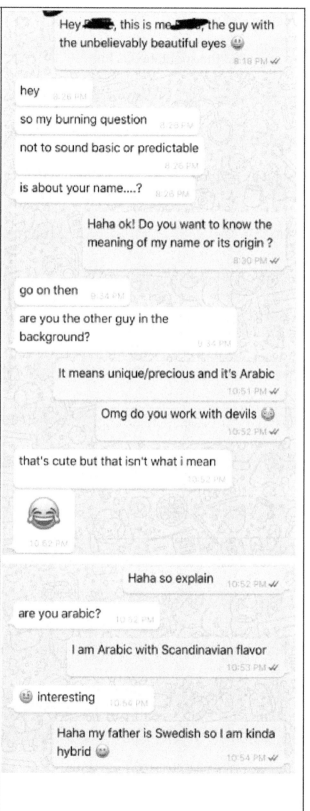

Hey ███, this is me ███ the guy with the unbelievably beautiful eyes 😃
8:18 PM

hey 8:26 PM

so my burning question 8:26 PM

not to sound basic or predictable 8:26 PM

is about your name....? 8:26 PM

Haha ok! Do you want to know the meaning of my name or its origin ?
8:30 PM

go on then 8:34 PM

are you the other guy in the background?
8:34 PM

It means unique/precious and it's Arabic
10:51 PM

Omg do you work with devils 😊
10:52 PM

that's cute but that isn't what i mean
10:52 PM

😂
10:52 PM

Haha so explain 10:52 PM

are you arabic? 10:52 PM

I am Arabic with Scandinavian flavor
10:53 PM

😃 interesting 10:54 PM

Haha my father is Swedish so I am kinda hybrid 😃
10:54 PM

| She stopped responding because, before the phone number, he was efficient and fast. He was taking action. Now there is a bullshit conversation leading away from the original purpose. It is inconsistent. | can you not just say you're mixed race ?<br><br>Hahah I need to improve my English! Would you help me ? 10:55 PM |

| Someone's Messages | |
|---|---|
| | |
| Spontaneous line. | hey girl, let's skip the boring part of those conversations, how spontaneous are you? |
| | Today 10:14 |
| She needs clarification. | Do you mean if I am spontaneous enough to meet you? |
| | Today 10:40 |
| This is literally, why the spontaneous opener and the adventurous opener are so great. It puts you in the judgement chair and makes you screen her first instead of her screen you. | just trying to find out whether you are fun to hang out with |
| | Well it depends what you consider as fun :) |
| | But I would say yes 😊 |
| | for example playing catch in the city XD |
| Three things line. | tell me what three things we should do when we meet |
| | It is funny. It like a test. Not sure if I like it |
| | Well I have moved here three weeks ago. So I don't know. |
| | But I would start with ice cream because ice cream it is always a good start |
| Now you know what she wants to get up to. | And then some food because I would want to get drunk really quickly |
| | And then find the best gin and tonic in the town |
| | It is hard to say just we should do what we would feel like doing |
| | It is hard to plan this things |
| | Maybe ask some pain the streets |

| Someone's Messages | |
|---|---|
| Spontaneous line. | Today 17:28 |
| | hey girl. let's skip the boring part of those conversations. how spontaneous are you? |
| | I don't know) |
| | Hi |
| | Today 17:47 |
| | then we definitely need to find out |
| 3 things line. | what three things should we do when we meet? |
| | Hug laugh admire |
| | What do u think? |
| | I think that sounds like a beautiful plan |
| Phone number. | do you have whatsapp? |
| | +38 |
| Summary: SIMPLIFY. | |

# Timing: How Long Should You Wait?

Ask yourself. *'How long should I wait?'*

Don't be that desperate guy who responds to a girl the second she sends you a message. There is only one situation in which you should respond in very quick time, and that is if you are meeting at that moment and you are trying to look for each other. Alternatively, if it is another time-sensitive matter where she, for example, wants to come over spontaneously but needs you to confirm if that is okay. If she is meeting you that day and asks if 8PM is a good time, you should obviously respond before it's too late. The definition of 'too late' in this case is 8PM, minus the amount of time it takes her to get ready as well as the time of travel, as well as extra time for the sake of not rushing her. A 7PM confirmation for a meeting time of 8PM is a rush, but confirming hours before is very comfortable. When it comes to solidifying a time, that is absolutely the final step you need to take in the message game, so it does not quite matter how quick you are to confirm with each other when the meet up will take place, as long as it is comfortably before the meeting takes place. That's the issue of time-sensitivity.

The main issue, of course, is that many guys do not know how long they should wait for literally anything. If you get a  match on Tinder, you can message straight away. Most girls do not send the first message. Useless! Sexism! But it is of course a good opportunity for you to message her minutes after matching, in case she wants to say something first that she has been meaning to say. You never really know if she wants to message you first, but that does not matter. Just send it. However, when it comes to timing in relation to receiving replies and when you should view their messages or respond to them, you should not be responding straight away or in a matter of minutes. I will break it down for you so you can picture it.

If a girl messages you out of nowhere, then you can reply without worrying about timing; it does not matter if it is a few minutes or a few hours. If a girl messages you because you sent her a message, then she is responding to your message. If she is responding immediately, you have nothing to worry about if you respond immediately in this case. If she responds after 10 minutes, do not respond to her immediately, do not respond to her in 5 minutes, do not respond to her in 10 minutes. If she responds after one hour, do not respond to her immediately, do not respond to her in 10 minutes, do not respond to her in 30 minutes. If she takes an entire day to reply, do not reply that day. You should wait at least 150% of the time she took in the case of up to a few hours as a general, but loose, rule. It's not black and white, just recommended. Even if she takes two years to reply, don't take 3 years to reply; that would be a massive waste of time. But just be sure that your timing does not imply that you do not have things going on in your life or that you are really bored and just need attention from girls on Facebook or any other form of messaging or communicating. You can find out about people by everything they do; their timing, their words, their behavior, etc. In the sense of timing, if she responds fast then she is probably obsessed with you or really needs attention, but if she takes a   long time to reply, she probably has a lot of things to do or has a lot of messages, or does not pay much attention to her phone.

If you are both replying to each other fast, you really need to make it actually go somewhere and have a purpose. You are not reading this to learn how to collect pen pals, you are here to prevent that from happening and make dates happen, so you can gain new experiences, friends and relationships. Have a bit of pace. If you're falling in love with a girl over messages, you really need to reevaluate your existence. Just meet her.

Any pattern that occurs extremely frequently with minimal anomalies is a predictable pattern. If you are always responding very fast to girls even if they take long to reply, they can exploit that and they will also know that you will respond quickly; you're predictable. If you always take long to reply even if girls reply fast, they can call you out on that. They will therefore know very well that you take a long time to respond. However, this is less of a problem because you are in a position of power and can fix it by just saying that you were busy; just like any girl would say to creepy guys who ask girls why they are not responding and why they are not petting their poor lonely stalking creeps.

Optimally, the time it takes you to reply to someone should tell her that you have other girls to talk to and that you have a life and things to do. You should not respond quickly in excitement, especially if the girl you are responding to takes a long time to reply. If there is a girl who is very unresponsive, you need to go **onto the next** girl by having the abundance mindset of being able to interact with other girls; you should not be dependent on one girl. A common question often asked is along the lines of *'what if she says she is busy over the next two weeks? Should I keep it warm by keeping the conversation going?'* No. Come back to her when her busy period is over. You should have access to many options so that if one is less responsive, you can work on five other interactions.

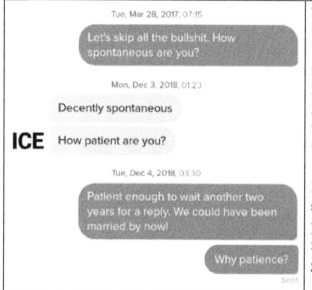

### Tinder

I sent this message on 28 March 2017. I received a reply 616 days later on 3 December 2018, almost 2 years, which is approximately 2% of the average human lifespan. I waited a very long time for this response, but my life went on.

I also replied the next day because it would be silly to wait another 2 years just to make a point. It took a long enough time for a response, so it is still worth a try at making it go somewhere soon.

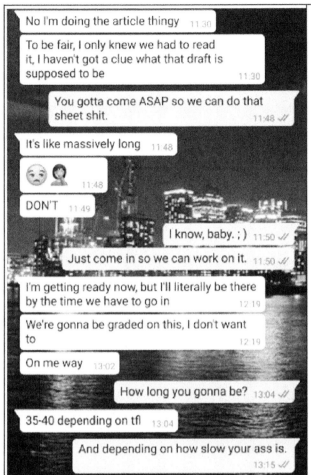

No I'm doing the article thingy 11:30

To be fair, I only knew we had to read it, I haven't got a clue what that draft is supposed to be 11:30

You gotta come ASAP so we can do that sheet shit. 11:48 ✓✓

It's like massively long 11:48

😩👩 11:48

DON'T 11:49

I know, baby. ; ) 11:50 ✓✓

Just come in so we can work on it. 11:50 ✓✓

I'm getting ready now, but I'll literally be there by the time we have to go in 12:19

We're gonna be graded on this, I don't want to 12:19

On me way 13:02

How long you gonna be? 13:04 ✓✓

35-40 depending on tfl 13:04

And depending on how slow your ass is. 13:15 ✓✓

## WhatsApp

This was about essays, so I decided to make it fun. It was also time-sensitive, so I was very sure to check in on when exactly she would arrive.

**Tinder**

She responded pretty fast, so I also checked up soon after at 18:32.

She responds at 21:00. At night there is no point responding if you have already waited for that reply, so it is often better to reply in the morning; then the whole day is ahead of her; she responded in the morning when I sent the message in the morning.

She then gave her phone number, but checked the conversation only two hours later to find she got one of the numbers wrong; she fixed it herself.

Patience will quite often serve you well, so do not rush.

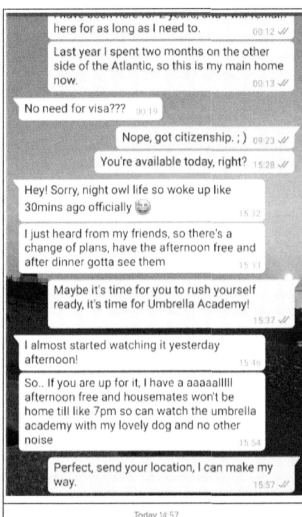

## WhatsApp

We were supposed to meet on this day, so it is time-sensitive. She sent me a message at 00:19 and I decided to sleep or do something else, saving my response in the morning until 09:23. She still did not come online, so I messaged again at 15:28 because it is time-sensitive.

At the time it felt like I had to rush, but luckily it was not a problem. She specified that we would be alone until 19:00, so this gives me good information that she would not have to interact with others.

So I made my way to her place, and by the time someone else came to the house we just moved to her room and I stayed the night with her.

## Tinder

It took her less than 4 hours to respond to my original message. If I replied too fast, it would not have escalated that quickly; she sent an additional message after less than 4 hours. In summary, don't rush to reply. She could chase you and skip the bullshit for you.

**WhatsApp**

In these first few messages I wanted her to come to my place. She isn't very good at communicating or meeting up.

But eventually this meant she had to do the rest of the work to see me again.

I went to the place.

I then had to leave after a few hours.

**WhatsApp**

She wanted to see me on Sunday.

She wanted to be sure. She must really like me. Big IOI.

04:24 in the morning, she has been out partying and she is horny and wants to have sex with me.

She is embarrassed, messages me again at 11:22 after I didn't say anything. Big IOI.

We met again and had sex.

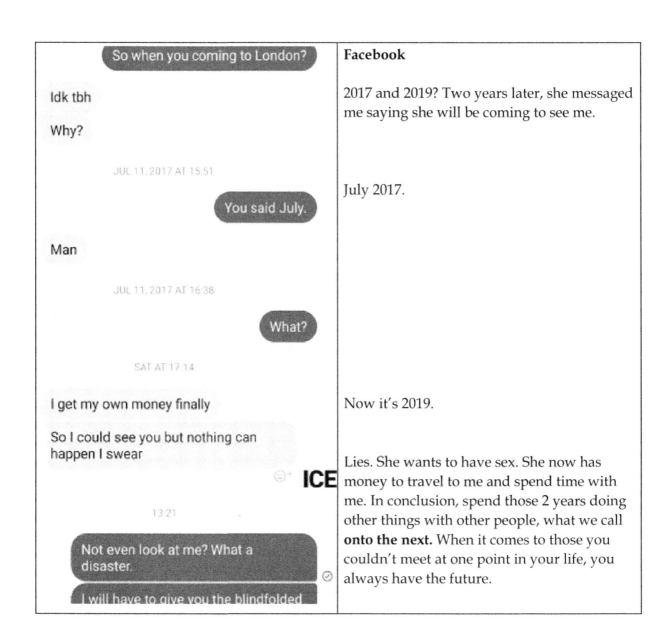

**Facebook**

2017 and 2019? Two years later, she messaged me saying she will be coming to see me.

July 2017.

Now it's 2019.

Lies. She wants to have sex. She now has money to travel to me and spend time with me. In conclusion, spend those 2 years doing other things with other people, what we call **onto the next.** When it comes to those you couldn't meet at one point in your life, you always have the future.

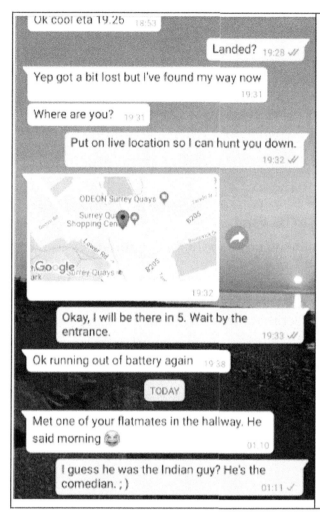

**WhatsApp**

A girl from Tinder was meeting me for the first time and running out of battery. Communication and precision is vital.

I can find her using a map.

We meet.

She had to leave early in the morning after having sex because she had to be at work.

# Timing Assignment

Your mission is to stick to the rules below. These are the rules of engagement that you should follow so that you do not appear to be desperate or bored. If you are new to this concept, you will stick to it very closely in your mind every time you see a message. Over time, your brain will be more automatic in working out when a good time to respond is.

1. Do not ask why a girl is not responding.
2. Do not ask a girl why she is taking long to respond.
3. Do not message a girl back immediately if she takes more than 2 minutes to send you a message.
4. Do not message a girl back in less time than she did unless it is a time-sensitive issue such as that you are supposed to meet that day or if she has not responded in many days, weeks, months, years or decades.

# Disclaimers: What If You Mess It Up?

The worst mistakes you have made in terms of sending messages are already over. You now know more, you ultimately won't make mistakes bigger than those you already made.

Remember, message game is for meeting, not for negotiating your way into a girl's pants, and not for trying to change her mind about whether or not she wants to have sex with you. Your goal is to meet and then take things from there; it is better to meet and to physically lead to sex than to message her to try to convince her to have sex with you. If she is not interested at any level, she will not meet you. If she meets you, that's a good sign and that's all you need to know; it is an IOI. If she messages you first, it is an IOI. If she is still talking to you, it is an IOI.

However, if she flakes on you or doesn't show up, then she is either not very interested in meeting you or not organized enough to remember she was supposed to meet you. Many guys get frustrated when a girl flakes, it is understandable. However, it is very important to remain unreactive and just go onto the next. You should have many females available for you to communicate with, so do not get stuck on one person. If she isn't very responsive towards you, then she is definitely not someone you should consider as special. If you haven't even met her, she is definitely not special. Do not get hung up over someone you have not met, and do not get hung up over someone who is not responsive. There are millions of other girls out there who could be so much better for you.

There are plenty of fish in the sea.

There will be another bus.

Onto the next.

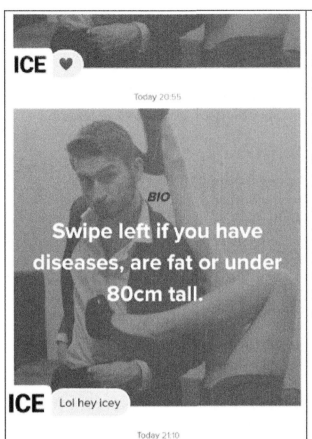

## Tinder

No matter what you do or what kind of person you are, not everyone will like you.

In this example, I did not get any messages from this woman until I changed my bio to something more provoking by mentioning fat people.

There is no right or wrong, you will never have the perfect profile for every single person on Tinder who sees it. People respond differently to various things, so it is important to let go of trying to please everyone.

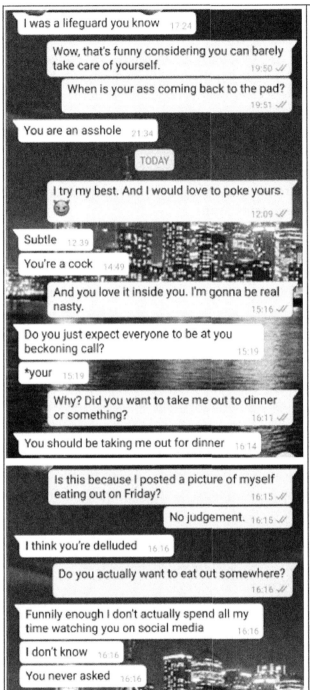

## WhatsApp

There is purpose straight away; I asked her when we would meet again. Pay attention to this fact; she did not resist. She called me an asshole, she called me a cock, but she did not resist.

She asked me if I just expect her to be at my beckoning call, but she did not resist.

Our relationship was mainly sexual. We did not spend time together outside of our own homes, but she put across the idea that I should want more. She seemingly wanted more.

I posted a photo on Instagram where I was having food with someone else. She saw it, and I was asking if she is upset because of that. If she is, then she wants a relationship.

She avoids answering, but I genuinely ask her if she wants to. She said she doesn't know, but that is okay; in such a situation this means that she is either confused about her feelings or just hesitant.

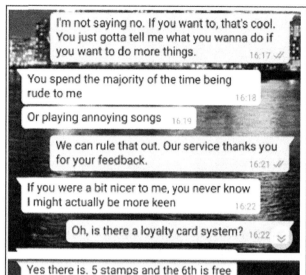

I'm not saying no. If you want to, that's cool. You just gotta tell me what you wanna do if you want to do more things. 16:17

You spend the majority of the time being rude to me 16:18

Or playing annoying songs 16:19

We can rule that out. Our service thanks you for your feedback. 16:21

If you were a bit nicer to me, you never know I might actually be more keen 16:22

Oh, is there a loyalty card system? 16:22

Continued.

So I was then clear to her in my next message that she can express whatever she wants to, I make it clear that it is not a big deal to say what she wants and that I am paying attention to what she wants.

The rest of the conversation is less meaningful, but many messages on we eventually found time to meet again.

Yes there is. 5 stamps and the 6th is free 16:22

Yes 16:24

Okay, so let's just chill out. No more annoying each other. We can be on an equal level, because you have rights. Okay? 16:27

Fine. 16:28

Fair. 16:28

You can wear whatever you want. Personally, I get really turned on by lingerie and find that very sexy. And if you ever do that for me again, I will make it definitely worth a lot to you too. 16:29

♡ ⭕ Reply

What's this

> That is a screaming cat on a pair of pants.

Bring me to backstage

Today 4:46 PM

> There are some rules first. Say please.

please

Dear sweetie lovely adorable ice white, can you bring me to back stage? Please

> Say 'please daddy'.

## Instagram

This did not work. But she still met me multiple times in the space of a few weeks after this, and she also kept calling me from time to time for many months.

The key here is that I had a valuable thing she wanted to experience; I had something interesting to offer. That was the fact that I could take her backstage in a large club and venue in front of thousands of people. I can use that as advantage instead of giving away my power easily.

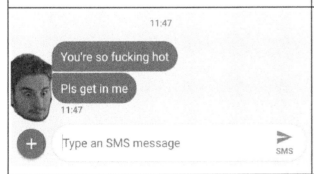

## SMS

If she is very clear about what she wants, then you should have nothing to worry about. If none of you are clear about what each of you want, perhaps some direction needs to be shown in your conversation.

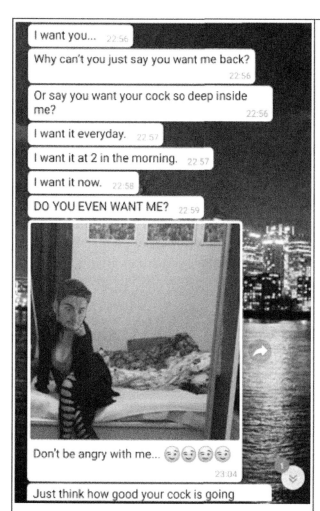

**WhatsApp**

She is obsessed. Maybe one time you used to be a little like this, now you can be on the other side of it.

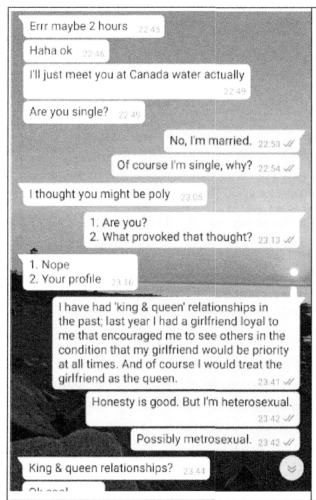

## WhatsApp

This was a discussion the night before we met; a girl I matched with on Tinder.

The plans for meeting were already set. She asked if I am single. I gave a non-serious answer to lighten up the conversation, and responded in a very clear way as if her question was silly; but most importantly I asked her why she asked so I would know how she thinks.

My prediction was right; I knew that she asked this question based on my photos from Tinder and possibly Instagram because some of the photos involve girls.

I then explained that I am open to seeing multiple girls at the same time.

We had sex the next day, and that was the first day we actually met.

| | **Tinder** |
|---|---|
| *Wednesday 22:17* | |
| Let's skip all the bullshit. How adventurous are you? | Line sent. |
| *Wednesday 22:45* | |
| ICE That depends, in what context? | Clarity needed. |
| *Wednesday 23:01* | |
| Put it this way, what 3 things would you love to do for our first date? | Reframed to capture her thoughts on what would be great things to do. |
| *Wednesday 23:44* | |
| ICE 1. Go to a theme park and go on the scariest rides<br>2. Go to a crazy rave night somewhere<br>3. Getting in a car or on the train and going some place neither of us have visited before and hoping for the best | She seems quite adventurous and fun. |
| I was thinking of that third one. Let's go to Copenhagen, Manchester or something. ; ) That would be one hell of a story. | The third one is the craziest and would be an amazing life story, so I take it as a very real opportunity. |
| *Today 00:21* | |
| ICE Yeah I like number 3<br>Best way to get to know someone; take yourselves away from everything you know<br>But there's the small issue of my passport, it's expired so I can only go as far as this country for now.<br>But that's fine, there's plenty of places I've never been to in this country before | She agrees and is very serious about it. She also states that her passport has expired. Being an English citizen, she can access Wales and Scotland without showing ID, which are the only countries we can therefore go to without a passport renewal. |
| *Today 00:37* | |
| Perfect, I feel the same way. I have never been to Manchester or Edinburgh before, so there are two good options. Got WhatsApp? | Now it is time to move to WhatsApp and make something amazing happen; going to another country for a first date. |
| ICE I've never been to Manchester or Edinburgh either so we can definitely put those in the hat to choose from.<br>Yes I have WhatsApp<br>07 ICE ICE | She complies. |

150

## WhatsApp

This is the same girl from the page before, so here is an extremely useful continuation of the conversation in this case study. My name is stated to clarify that it's me. I also put forward that there is no way we can miss the opportunity to travel together for a first date.

It is only 4 hours to Manchester from London and 10 hours to Edinburgh from London. I have spent entire days travelling across North America, so it does not bother me.

She states when she will be available to book everything.

Blah blah blah.

She qualifies herself, which shows even more as an IOI that she is definitely into it.

Setting the plan in detail.

**Logistics** stated.

Location sent.

Blah blah blah.

Time to go.

She is coming.

By now she has proven to be very reliable at communicating and letting me know details of timing. This is extremely beneficial and attractive to me since this is about doing something quite different, edgy and dangerous.

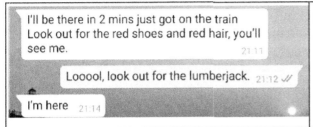

She also makes it clear for me as to what I should look out for; her communication is very solid.

We met that night and booked the trip for our first date. A very real adventure.

**WhatsApp**

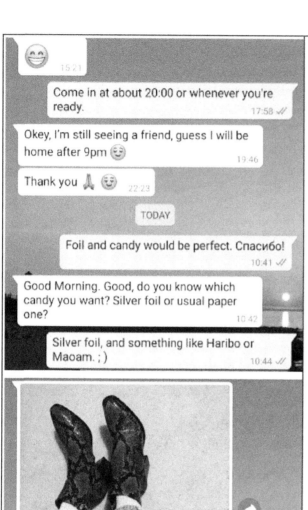

Come in at about 20:00 or whenever you're ready.  17:58

Okey, I'm still seeing a friend, guess I will be home after 9pm 😌  19:46

Thank you 🙏 😌  22:23

TODAY

Foil and candy would be perfect. Спасибо!  10:41

Good Morning. Good, do you know which candy you want? Silver foil or usual paper one?  10:42

Silver foil, and something like Haribo or Maoam. ; )  10:44

Watching TV shows together.

She asked if I wanted anything from the store.

She bought these for me.

Check out my sexy yellow socks.. I borrowed them from Aleksandra  20:30

Feeling like Bart Simpson  20:30

I'm digging those shoes too, dayum. That's hot.  20:32

Come in when you're ready for the next episode.  20:33

We are going out now with Aleksandra, maybe I will come in later.. depends how long I will be gone 🐻  20:33

She is focusing on the socks, but really she might want me to see her shoes.

I reward her for showing me.

We saw each other another time.

# Dealing With Rejection: Why Is She Ignoring You?

So ask yourself. *'Why is she ignoring me?'*

There can be many reasons why someone is ignoring you. One of the most common ones is that you're just being annoying. Stop it. Seriously.

Are you a man or a bitch? If you are offended by some girl you have never met or that you barely know, you can go shrivel up like your wrinkly little penis does in the cold. Never be reactive towards a girl if she ignores you, rejects you or says something negative. Never fall into her frame when this happens either. If you are offended so easily, go cry in a corner while everyone else makes better use of their time.

## WhatsApp

I'm not a girl, but I received these messages. I do not know who this guy is. I do not know the phone number. The person does not even have a photo. Needless to say, do not be this guy.

On top of all that, this person did not mention who he is. He did not say his name. He did not say why he is messaging me. He did not say how he acquired my phone number.

Ultimately, none of this appears to have any purpose. It is needy. It is obsessive. It is unnecessary and annoying.

Imagine how many times a girl has to put up with this. There is no way you can expect to achieve anything by acting this way.

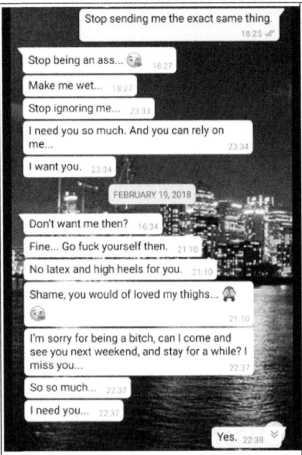

## WhatsApp

Ignoring girls to some extent can make them even more needy and desperate, giving you higher value.

Over the course of 28 hours, she did not receive any response from me, but she left me 12 messages begging for my attention and also literally begging for sex.

## SMS

Time is often something that people forget about. It is a variable in everything we do that never seems to be clear in terms of what could happen.

In this case, time will show me that she is desperate and obsessed, and she will be more likely to admit or communicate relatively clearly what she wants and how she feels.

I'm becoming very sexually confident around you. *14:44*

Isn't he adorable *20:14*

TODAY

Good. I like confident. *10:40*

And what did you think of my dog *12:48*

Your dog? I thought that was a video of you from Snapchat. *15:48*

Number one you don't have me on snapchat *15:49*

Number two I do not look black and fluffy *15:50*

Number three I want to ride you on my sofa *15:50*

1. Number 3 should be at the top of your list.

2. That's it. *15:51*

Aha, I agree. Come round on Thursday and let me seduce you. *15:52*

And ride you *15:52*

## WhatsApp

At 14:44, she stated that she is becoming sexually confident around me. 5 hours and 30 minutes after no response, she sent a video of a dog.

I responded to her message, but not the message about the dog. She then wanted me to respond to her about the dog, only for me to make a joke out of it by effectively calling her a dog.

She then become more sexual by saying that she wants to ride me on her sofa after she talks about two other points. I ignore the first two points and address her third one, without even being sexual.

She then tried to lure me in for sex and told me when to come.

Continued.

I told her to keep talking, as she is very invested into being sexual with me already. She goes through the steps, and I simply say that I like it.

She then offered to also cook for me, at this point I started replying after even longer periods of time.

Finally, she wants to know if I will stay for the night. Her intentions are clear, and my messaging was very minimal and effortless. Everything mentioned happened that week, only that the food was not that interesting.

You can also see a preview message here at the end to show what her next response was; admitting that she just looks forward to the sex. The original Message Game Guide (2018) featured a chapter like this.

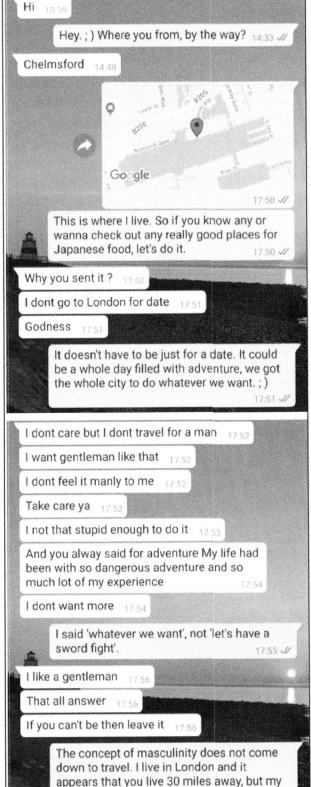

Hi 13:35

Hey. ;) Where you from, by the way? 14:33

Chelmsford 14:48

This is where I live. So if you know any or wanna check out any really good places for Japanese food, let's do it. 17:50

Why you sent it ? 17:50

I dont go to London for date 17:51

Godness 17:51

It doesn't have to be just for a date. It could be a whole day filled with adventure, we got the whole city to do whatever we want. ;) 17:51

I dont care but I dont travel for a man 17:52

I want gentleman like that 17:52

I dont feel it manly to me 17:52

Take care ya 17:52

I not that stupid enough to do it 17:53

And you alway said for adventure My life had been with so dangerous adventure and so much lot of my experience 17:54

I dont want more 17:54

I said 'whatever we want', not 'let's have a sword fight'. 17:55

I like a gentleman 17:56

That all answer 17:56

If you can't be then leave it 17:56

The concept of masculinity does not come down to travel. I live in London and it appears that you live 30 miles away, but my radius is set to 6 miles. 17:56

## WhatsApp

This was a continuation over WhatsApp from a match on Tinder. I sent her my location and gave a plan to start from.

Immediately she reacted in a 'princess' way. Her behavior using certain words and phrases such as 'I don't' , 'I don't [do something] for a man' , 'I want a gentleman [who would do something that I would not do for them]' and much more to follow. This behavior is what I call the princess mentality - where the girl expects the guy to do everything. I also call this sexism. It is not a good sign, and I certainly do not want to have a relationship with someone like that.

Her reaction also paved her way into explaining why she was triggered, she shows fear by mentioning 'dangerous' adventures she had.

On top of all this, she also says another line of the princess mentality 'if you can't be.' This is an expectation she has of whom she is talking to, think about it rephrased as 'if you can't be [up to my expectations]' or 'if you can't be [up to my standards]'. By expecting too much of people in such a sexist way, she will not have success in dating. In each case, I have seen of this, most women with this exact behavior have been above the age of 25. So ironically, these people will most likely die alone if they do not change.

The inevitable flaw of the princess mentality is that any man that falls for it just becomes her bitch.

You are then one want adventure then only 30 miles 17:57

That scared 17:57

Omg hahaha 17:57

So quite simply, you have been here before and you will most likely be here again. 17:57 ✓✓

What ? 17:57

I dont going to travel for men 17:58

I'm not ordering you to travel just for me. 17:58 ✓✓

You're not a pizza. 17:58 ✓✓

That men job to show how gentlemen they are 17:58

Hey 17:58

IM clear now 17:58

Leave it ok 17:58

? 17:58

Continued.

Plus, of course, lots of what she writes makes no sense. The way I respond is very calm and simple, it is unreactive. Whereas her behavior is reactive and all over the place.

The final princess line is 'it is a man's job'. This behavior probably means that she would expect you to pay for her food when you eat out with her or her drinks when you go to a club or a bar. Maybe it even means she will also expect you to buy her clothes. On another level, if you get married, she would probably eventually divorce you and take your money and your house. This behavior at even a low level may extend to such long-term extremes.

To summarize, it's good that she blocked me. Dodged a bullet.

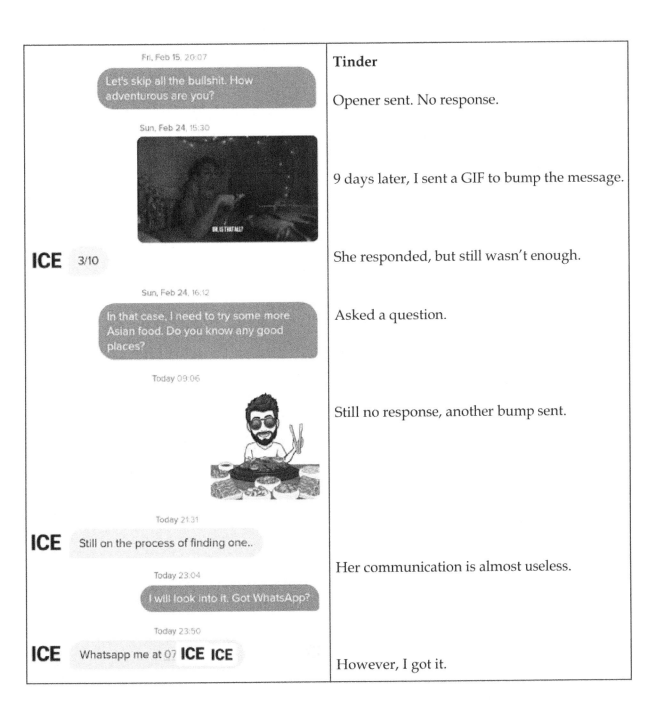

## Tinder

Opener sent. No response.

9 days later, I sent a GIF to bump the message.

She responded, but still wasn't enough.

Asked a question.

Still no response, another bump sent.

Her communication is almost useless.

However, I got it.

**ICE**

Thursday 21:05

U match girls so they out their shoes in your face for ig?

Today 18:15

If you would love to do that, then the answer can become yes from my answer of no.

I'm just here to meet people. ; ) So my question is... What are three things we should do for a first date? Having your shoes in my face can be one if you want.

Today 19:24

Confusing answers

I go ond dates with ppl I already know and met once

Not so keen in meeting you

But I'm just wondering what the heck do you do

Why the girls shoes and the ego

**ICE**

Today 21:06

You must be fun at parties? Does my beard or lumberjack look scare you?

You're wondering what I do, in terms of magically having such photos, or in terms of money laundering?

Don't ever ask me about my ego, I would be forced to declare that my IQ is above room temperature. Anyway, what's your obsession with that girl and her shoes?

Seen

**Tinder**

She opened. Interesting but weird question referring to one of my photos on Instagram, inspired by a scene in The Wolf Of Wall Street where Jordan Belfort is tempted by his wife taking her panties off.

Well, she's a mean one.

Accuses me of ego, quite hypocritical and quite the opposite.

I sent a load of lighthearted joking messages.

She unmatched. Her loss and perhaps something I can learn from. Perhaps it is better not to justify or explain yourself, especially to someone who communicates with an ego and from a frame of disagreement.

| | |
|---|---|
| 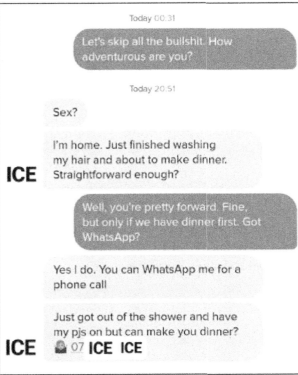 Today 00:31<br><br>Let's skip all the bullshit. How adventurous are you?<br><br>Today 20:51<br><br>Sex?<br><br>**ICE** I'm home. Just finished washing my hair and about to make dinner. Straightforward enough?<br><br>Well, you're pretty forward. Fine, but only if we have dinner first. Got WhatsApp?<br><br>Yes I do. You can WhatsApp me for a phone call<br><br>**ICE** Just got out of the shower and have my pjs on but can make you dinner?<br>🔒 07 **ICE  ICE** | **Tinder**<br><br>Adventurous line sent.<br><br>Assumption.<br><br><br><br><br>I accuse her of wanting sex instead of letting her accuse me.<br><br><br><br>Got it. She was not very good at communicating through WhatsApp, so I did not proceed further. |
|  Ice. ; ) 21:13<br>I would love dinner, madame. 21:13<br>Good 21:13<br>And your name is 21:13<br>I C E 21:13<br>In case of emergency? 21:14<br>Cute bye 21:14<br>No. 21:14<br>It's my real name. 21:14<br>You suddenly hate me because you don't like white people now? Racist! 21:15 | **WhatsApp**<br><br>When receiving her phone number, I sent her my name and continued the conversation so she knows who I am and what to save me as.<br><br><br>Because she doesn't understand my name and is therefore inconsiderate and quite dumb, I decided to explain it. Then I joked with her. She blocked me. Her loss. If she is to act in such a way, then she definitely would not be good enough for me; you also must believe in this idea. |

Today 22:35

> Let's skip all the bullshit. How adventurous are you?

Probably more then you

> That's curious. Flex. What did you do that compares to my power?

I just look cooler 😄

You're not really my type but nice YouTube channel

> Maybe, but in fairness if you gave me the look you give in your last photo I would probably be on my knees like Danny in Grease when Sandy spices herself up.

Shut up

Im watching your videos

Are you a masochist public speaker?

> No, I teach people about dating, lifestyle and communication.

> That's a funny question you got there.

> I hope you at least subscribed so you can do more stalking.

Just seen masochist photos on insta, you say everything on your profile

And I'm bored, had to stalk everywhere

It's missing a bit of mistery there

> You mean the photo of a girl in high heels basically kicking my head? I guess you haven't seen The Wolf Of Wall Street.

---

**Tinder**

Adventurous line sent.

It's a competition, apparently.

She already Googled me and searched everywhere for me. She's coming from an intimidation frame, not a good start.

I try to lighten it up.

She is distracted and still researching me instead of communicating with me like a real nice person would.

I accuse her of stalking playfully.

She doesn't understand masochism and is exaggerating something she saw in one photo inspired by a scene from The Wolf Of Wall Street.

It's like she is analyzing and critiquing my profiles.

| | |
|---|---|
| Still masochist 😔 | Doesn't understand masochism or The Wolf Of Wall Street. |
| That's really not masochist. I'm a dominant person and that was just a photoshoot that involved all kinds of different scenes. Why? Do you like being a pain in the ass? ;) | |
| So you're pretending to me then ! Hahah was just asking. Good luck on your tinder! 😳 | Obviously isn't interested. Wasting my time. |
| Wow, lady. This isn't a mission to Mars. This has been too interesting not to pursue, do you have WhatsApp? I guess you already found me on Facebook, Instagram, MySpace, Skype and Netflix already. ;) | I try to see where I can take it at least. |
| Im afraid you said on your video that telephones shouldn't be given haha | She also misunderstands more things from my profiles, and more basic words. |
| WhatsApp is not telephone, and I said nothing about telephones. This isn't 1986. As a general rule, it is better to connect on social media with people you meet, but there is an exception for online dating; where it is better to take it to WhatsApp instead. | |
| So cute that you're learning already. ;) | Teaching her knowledge. |
| I don't give my WhatsApp like that, but you can follow me on Instagram as i need more engagement 😔 | Time for me to come from a higher frame to put her below. |
| A ICE ‹x | |
| Do you have Facebook? It's not like I'm gonna call you on WhatsApp and listen to you cry about Avengers. ;) | She just wants me to follow her. |
| Noooo | I refuse. |
| Insta is better o need more followers | She desperately wants followers. |

I need*

Im poor in the likes section and in the followers as well

Hahahaha

> Let's just go crazy and do everything, Facebook, Instagram and WhatsApp.

Trying hard.

Instagram is just fine 😄

> Then go follow me, rude! ; ) I forgot to throw in YouTube, let's also subscribe to each other and merge Netflix accounts.

I still try to see where I can take it.

Hahahahahaha great!

> Facebook: Icey White
> Instagram: IceWhiteOfficial
> WhatsApp: +447 **ICE ICE**
> Now gimme your Netflix login!

She still is just trying to get followers, but still hasn't followed me despite stalking me. Standards must be set. I won't fall for her that easy.

Ahhhhhhh

You want a free Netflix account isn't it?

I give her my details, and a joke.

Hahahahahaha

Im not giving anything, you didn't even follow me on Instagram

Im hurt now

> I already have Netflix.

Expecting me to follow her, yet she has not followed me. This is why Instagram is not solid for closing; too much ego is involved on Instagram.

> You didn't follow me. So I bet you didn't even subscribe either. You're so mean.

I did!

I go on further and she tries to qualify herself.

I followed even on YouTube

| | |
|---|---|
| Okay, just a little bit of my faith in you has been restored. | She followed me on Instagram. As predicted, it went absolutely nowhere. |
| Hahahaha | |
| **Tinder** Tue, Jan 24, 2017, 20:01 Let's skip all the bullshit. How spontaneous are you? | **Tinder** Spontaneous line sent in January 2017. |
| Tue, Jan 24, 2017, 21:58 Pretty damn spontaneous | |
| Tue, Jan 24, 2017, 22:55 Pretty damn good then. You free tomorrow? | Is she free tomorrow? |
| Today 19:48 I'm wet, horny and in need of some dirty talk | Apparently not, she replied over 2 years later. It is May 2019, and I am not falling for that. |
| I'm hungry, horny and have waited 2 years for you. Got WhatsApp? | |
| I don't, but nothing stopping us talking on here. I want hardcore dirty talk for me to wank to, you up for it? | She just wants to talk dirty, but I do not. I want dates. |
| Tell me what you'd do to me if you were in my bed right now | |
| I would slap your ass and make you download WhatsApp. | |
| Sent | WhatsApp or go away. All or nothing. Date or nothing. |

| | Tinder |
|---|---|
| Sun, Mar 24, 10:46 | |
| Let's skip all the bullshit. How adventurous are you? | Adventurous line sent. |
| Sun, Mar 24, 11:02 | |
| Compared to what exactly | |
| A lettuce, very | |
| Action man, not that adventurous | |
| Slightly right of Christopher Columbus on the adventureometer | |
| Mon, Mar 25, 14:51 | |
| Wow, you are one adventurous lettuce pirate explorer. If I say there is no limit, what are 3 things we should do for our first date? Anything. ; ) | I respond. |
| Today 19:41  | Still nothing, so I sent a GIF. |
| Today 20:21 | |
| Sorry I'm crap at tinder | |
| And also very busy and important | |
| You can tell by the hats | |
| Well I thought I was busy, damn. I have been across a few countries since then. ; ) Got WhatsApp, madame? | She reveals she doesn't pay attention to Tinder, so now it is WhatsApp or nothing. Sometimes people are genuinely busy, this is why fast moves are important. |
| Today 21:39 | |
| I do | |
| 07 **ICE ICE** | Collected. |

# Solving Problems: What Can You Do About It?

So ask yourself. *'What can I do about it?'*

Be a man and fucking deal with it.

From years of seeing other people's messages and receiving their questions, it was quite common to see people stressed out about when a girl changes her plans to meet. Some girls have cancelled on guys. Some girls have suddenly had a genuine change of plans because of family, work issues or anything else. Life gets in the way of many people, but there is no need to worry. What can you do about it if she is not available?

To start with, the average lifespan of a person is roughly 28,000 days, and most of you who are reading this right now most likely will not die this week, this month, or this year. In other words… You have time. Plenty of it. If she is not available on a particular day, you have other days in the future to choose. If you manage to secure a time, but then she has to cancel it or change it closer to when the d ate takes place, you still have the future. Yes, it can be frustrating to have changes to your plans because of other people, but there is nothing you can do about it. Instead, what you can do is embrace the fact that you and her are both, in most cases, going to live beyond the short-term realities of the right-now. There have been times that I did not see certain girls or go on a d ate, or in some cases another date, with her until weeks, months or even over a year later. Anything can happen, just make sure you are always still connected; as in you always have a w ay of contacting her at any time.

If you are struggling to find time with someone, you absolutely must not keep messaging that person at all times. You should only be messaging people out of necessity and meaning. If you had a romance with a   tourist or as a tourist and one of you had to leave and go somewhere else geographically, and if she was a great connection to you, it does not mean you should be messaging each other every day. You are not pen pals. This is not a high school love story romance where you will one day hope to reunite and fall in love, or at least definitely not if you are constantly trying to communicate; let it go. You can get back to that person at any time when you find a purpose to once again, and the best example of this is if you will both be geographically close a gain.

One time I met an amazing girl from California. I met her in Europe, but she was leaving the next day. We had an amazing time, but we had to say goodbye. We found each other on Facebook so that we could still be quite easily connected. One year later, I was travelling through some American states, so she was able to see that I was in her country at the same time as her. We checked in with each other, but she would be in California and I would be in New York, but we did at least try to see if we could meet. Another year went by, and we had still not found each other again, but I still have not finished travelling, just as I have still not finished living. No matter how long it takes, we could find each other again. There is no need to message her until one of us knows that we could quite easily meet again, but that requires that we would know we would be in the same place at the same time. Stay connected on Facebook, for example, but do not become pen pals. Do not ruin your connection by wearing it out on a screen that is brighter than your future.

On the other side, do not worry if you no longer like a particular girl or if a particular girl is no longer into you, or just ignores or blocks you. In very few cases, it will happen no matter what you do, it's the same as falling out with friends. Things change, do not be attached to certain people, or that will be considered obsessive. If one person no longer wants to talk to you, that is their loss. You do not need to cry about it, you do not need to react to it, you just need to move on; to the next person or to other people. There are billions of people out there, just because circumstances have changed with one person doesn't mean it is the end. Onto the next.

**Facebook**

Can't come. But, really, she can.

People make excuses very easily, it is important to realize that. So be equipped with being able to solve problems, like I solved this problem in one sentence.

She came to my place that day, as did two other girls. I slept with one of the three girls, and then slept with this girl 2 days later.

## Tinder

This conversation was not short enough, but it did the job.

Fri, Feb 10, 22:06

Let's skip all the bullshit. How spontaneous are you?

Fri, Feb 10, 22:55

8/10 I would say

Fri, Feb 10, 23:34

Spontaneity is now an Olympic sport?

Rate pizza.

20/10

The perfect response

You win.

Pizza goodness will come to you.

That is your fortune cookie prophecy.

Yesss thank you

My life is complete.

The problem I faced was that GIFs kept crashing my phone due to Tinder bugs. So I admitted that, and she actually thought it was a pickup line. It was actually the truth, but she loved it anyway.

These GIFs keep crashing my Tinder. Let's WhatsApp instead. Got a number?

Is that a pick up line

Cause it's working

The line is working? It's not even a line, I don't use lines. 😁

It's probably just my phone fucking up.

Problem solved, I have her number instead of messaging her on an app that keeps crashing.

So you don't want my phone number? 😊

07

**Tinder**

This screenshot begins at my second message to her.

When I ask for phone numbers, I tend to use the word 'WhatsApp' instead of the phrase 'phone number' because the latter phrase is more associated to sleazy guys trying to get phone numbers. I also ask it in the form of a closed question. Who the hell does not have a phone number?

Given that not everyone with a phone number has WhatsApp, WhatsApp is still a highly popular phone number-associated app that most people have. So in almost every single case I have personally come across, the answer is always 'yes', but normally it is communicated just by providing the phone number itself.

If she only says 'yes' and the phone number is not given, all you have to do is give the little push.

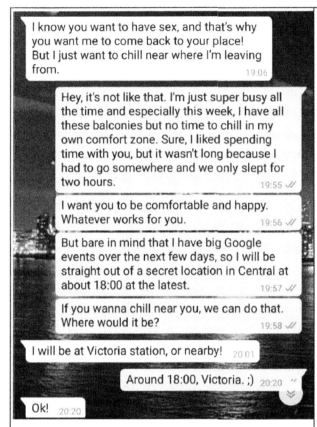

I know you want to have sex, and that's why you want me to come back to your place! But I just want to chill near where I'm leaving from. 19:06

Hey, it's not like that. I'm just super busy all the time and especially this week, I have all these balconies but no time to chill in my own comfort zone. Sure, I liked spending time with you, but it wasn't long because I had to go somewhere and we only slept for two hours. 19:55

I want you to be comfortable and happy. Whatever works for you. 19:56

But bare in mind that I have big Google events over the next few days, so I will be straight out of a secret location in Central at about 18:00 at the latest. 19:57

If you wanna chill near you, we can do that. Where would it be? 19:58

I will be at Victoria station, or nearby! 20:01

Around 18:00, Victoria. ;) 20:20

Ok! 20:20

## WhatsApp

This woman was a tourist in London that I had sex with when we met. These messages were from the day before she had to leave the city, and I wanted to see her one last time before she left.

She thought that I just wanted sex. Because she is in her 30s, she is an older woman and therefore it is more straightforward to communicate with her, so I openly talked her through it to give her comfort.

After her message at 20:01, I called her. Voice-to-voice is a great way to solve problems. I simply talked her through the plan step by step to relieve her of her worries that she would miss her transport, and she was happy. We would only have 3 hours to hang out.

Come the next day, we spent those last 3 hours together and it included sex. Everyone was happy.

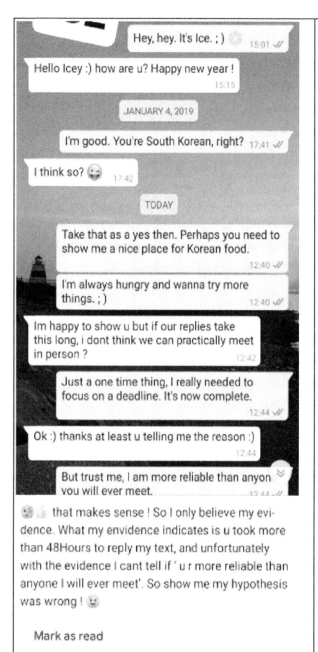

## WhatsApp

Just a few messages and she is already concerned about how long it takes me to respond to her; 48 hours. She questioned whether I would be reliable enough to meet her without causing inconvenience, so I had to provide her comfort by showing her that it is nothing to worry about.

Her insecurities were settled and I simply re-emphasized that she has nothing to worry about.

Her last message shown here, as the preview, shows that she specifically looked at how long exactly it took me to reply, which shows that she really cares. With this message she decided to be quite playful.

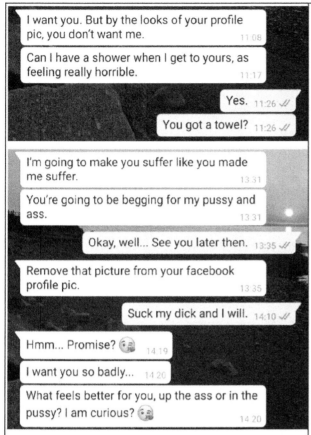

**WhatsApp**

She wants a relationship, but she is also desperate to have sex with me.

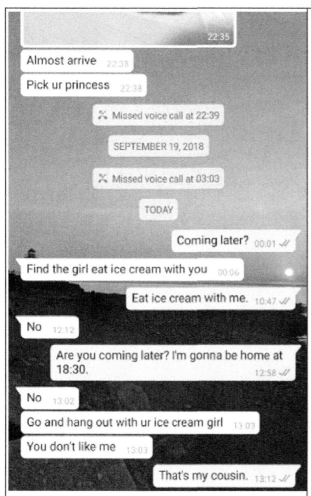

## WhatsApp

I often post my dates onto my stories on Facebook, Instagram and Snapchat; this all brings me social proof and preselection because when girls see that I am spending time with girls, then it is pretty apparent that I am already approved of by other girls. If we take the reverse; if a guy was never seen with any girls, then a girl would have less reasons to trust that guy than to trust the guy who is already hanging out with girls. One guy seems lonely, the other guy seems to be making girls happy. What would a girl prefer?

This girl came to my place and then wanted to go out with me again a few days later. At the very beginning she knew about me seeing other girls. Sometimes she was a little reactive, but never actually cared because she would still message me or find me anyway, even months later.

TUE AT 19.10

**ICE** 🌐 ☆

TUE AT 19:46

> What time will you be there? We can get food before if you're up for that.

TUE AT 19:57

**ICE** Not sure yet what time..it's only Tuesday..Lol

TUE AT 20:25

> I lost the concept of time today. Anyway, be fashionable. ; )

**ICE** Time doesn't exist..Lol everything is purple🐸

WED AT 21:26

**ICE** Don't think I'll be able to come <u>Friday</u>.. I got another event to go to..I will see u next time😸 ↓

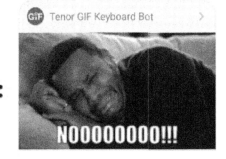

⚡ REPLY INSTANTLY

**ICE** Fuck off Mr White😼😎

**ICE** Have fun!! I surely will Friday🐸

**ICE** to Saturday till Sunday..Lol and Everyday ◐☺

🕐 · **ICE**

## Facebook

We arranged to go out on a Friday, but the next day she said that she may have to be somewhere else.

I dropped a sarcastic GIF with the intention for it to be funny.

She responded, but also gave some extra useless comments.

My final message to her was very sarcastic, but showed that I would check back on her another time so that we could rearrange. Therefore, the moral of the story is that you have your whole life ahead of you, you have thousands of possible days to choose to meet.

14:40

Okay, Miss Sunshineandrainbows. I will come to your magical purple forest another time and collect you for your journey to the West, where you can see the White Forest and the party of magic boob tricks and unicorns.

Do not be stressed out when your original plan gets changed, you can come back to her another time. You have the future. There are other girls out there. Onto the next.

---

You are now connected on Messenger.

TUE AT 17:08

That's not scary cosplay, that's cute as hell. 😌

TUE AT 18:02

Woaa that one was uncommon now ahahah

The lord satan thanks you 😺😺

TUE AT 21:51

Oh, you have no idea. I am Satan. I am the hand up Mona Lisa's skirt. I'm a surprise.

TUE AT 23:21

Hahahha satan club

WED AT 15:39

When is your next appearance at a cosplay event?

**Facebook**

We met in a university class, and when I mentioned Facebook she said that she does not give it out because, she claimed, it might be scary to people. Her Facebook profile was dedicated to cosplay.

Despite that, we connected on Facebook anyway. My first two messages were just playful, my third called for a meet up.

Unfortunately in the following days and weeks we never met up outside of that very university, but because she shared a mutual class with me, it meant that I would see her on a fairly regular basis anyway; so time can wait.

You wouldn't managed

Eh, you're a cute little kitten.

Perfect I will end up piggy back you knowing my luck

I can feed you little cat treats on the way

Or put you in a basket

Oi!

Anyway shouldn't you ask for my number just in case

Cuddles may be required

What is your number?

(Just in case) ; )

Who said I would give it to you when you ask! 😄😄😄

Can I ask you a question

This is the point where you joke around and give it to me anyway. : )

Yes

But I need a 100% honest answer

Yes

You didn't bet with guys from work that you will take me out or something

No way. I don't even talk about things like this, it should be between two people only.

Great thanks

Haha regarding my number

Well nope I rather not giving it to strangers lol

Eh, you're probably cheekier than me. ; )

And I will need to shoot off the latest for 22

## Facebook

One of my favorites of all time.

I met a woman at work and we instantly had an amazing connection and friendship. We would then message each other on Facebook while working; one thing led to another and we then arranged to do something together outside of the workplace.

She pushes across the idea that I should take her phone number, but first she asks if I made a bet with the people we know about taking her out. It is a call for comfort, and I settled her concern; it really wasn't a bet or anything like it. I was genuinely interested in her.

Most of the messages throughout are very playful, and responses are quick between both of us, which also shows not only that she is interested in me but also that I am, too, very interested in her. We just cannot wait.

As I have a dog

So he will be very unsettled

Give the dog to someone for the day. :)

No worries.

I wish I have noone

So what's your nr?

And me cheeky

Neverrrrr

Ooh, asking me now :)

Do you really deserve it?

Probably no and I will never do but hey

You live once hey

Right?!

It will take me like 2h to get back

I like that, so I'm gonna be a whore this time only and give it to you even though you are a stranger. ;)

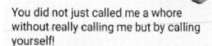

You did not just called me a whore without really calling me but by calling yourself!

Well I'm a    so not a stranger

She specified that she had to be back home at a certain time because of doggy responsibilities.

Proceeding through playfulness, she asked for my phone number. We then met outside of work, it rained, we ran to my house to hang out and play truth or dare and we made mojitos. One of the most random dates, but it was amazing, we had sex and we got into a relationship.

We always would spend our breaks at work together seemingly unintentionally or accidentally as if by magic, and I would personally get the butterflies in my stomach each time I saw her. We had the most amazing connection, and I have never experienced anything like that before or since. Unfortunately, months later we stopped seeing each other, we were at different stages in our lives.

| | |
|---|---|
| Tue, Feb 19, 22:36 | **Tinder** |
| Let's skip all the bullshit. How adventurous are you? | The first messages were about her saying that she thinks she has spoken to me before. This is the useless part. |
| Wed, Feb 20, 21:01 | |
| **ICE** I just a normal woman | |
| Thu, Feb 21, 14:46 | |
| Maybe it's tome to change or to get a non-normal milkshake. | |
| Thu, Feb 21, 23:21 | |
| **ICE** I think I've been chatting with you before | |
| Thu, Feb 21, 23:40 | |
| What do you mean? | |
| **ICE** I think we have chat before | |
| When? I don't remember you. | |
| **ICE** Don't know | Continuing from there, I said I do not remember her. |
| **ICE** Just feel like we had | |
| I call that magic. ; ) | |
| **ICE** I call voodoo | |
| That would mean that I'm controlling you. ; ) | |
| Fri, Feb 22, 13:04 | |
| **ICE** ??? | |
| Fri, Feb 22, 15:20 | |
| That's what voodoo magic does. Anyway, if you were to meet me, what is one thing you would like to do? (Activity/food/etc) | The conversation was not really going anywhere, so I used the 'anyway' card to give the conversation direction; leading it to meeting. |
| Monday 19:58 | |
| **ICE** Some where have a nice food | |

Continued.

She was compliant, but when choosing to move to WhatsApp she instead pointed out that on my Instagram profile I have pictures of other girls, so she thought I might already have a girlfriend.

To solve this, she just needs to know that these are photos of friends and that I in fact do not have a girlfriend; then it's not a problem. This is called 'comforting'.

Three days later, no response. So I poked at her again.

After telling her to name three things we should potentially eat, she just named one. Not very good at communicating.

Blah blah blah, now it is time for the second attempt to move this to WhatsApp and make the date happen.

Instead of giving me her number, she asked for mine, and then messaged me soon after.

This case was pretty different to others because there is a lot of messaging on her side that comes without focus or purpose.

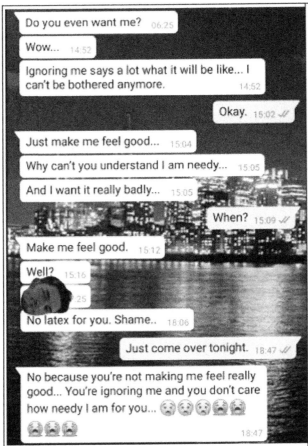

## WhatsApp

It's easy to say you will give up, just to not give up shortly after the declaration.

She can communicate relatively well, but she is terrible when it comes to meeting or focusing on the topic.

**Friday 16:34**

Let's skip all the bullshit. How adventurous are you?

Very!

**Sunday 11:24**

Wonderful, could you name 3 things that would be cool for us to do as a first date? ; )

**Sunday 15:12**

You first and what age are you?

**Sunday 18:36**

1. I am younger than you but I'm from the '80s and have dated older than you, so if you're comfortable, we're both comfortable.

Literally anything, no matter how crazy.

**Sunday 22:47**

What are you into ?

**Today 10:52**

I'm into food and seeing you in lingerie.

Oh sounds promising.. where are you based again?

Greenland Dock, Canada Water.

## Tinder

Adventurous line sent.

Not very compliant, now distracted by age.

Let's get her back on track.

Making a bolder move to get a feel for where I can take this.

She is asking more questions, so she is interested at least.

Today 12:46

Where are you based? And do you have WhatsApp?

I ask where she is, and she is relatively close.

Se24 and yes I have whatsapp but what age are you?

Distracted again.

Relax, it's okay. ; ) 29, what's your number?

OMG I'm actually 44 I'm too old for you

Age gap. I don't care.

Don't put yourself down like that. Funny enough, that still wouldn't be my oldest. I honestly don't mind. Okay?

I try to comfort her and say it makes no difference. No judgement.

Well apparently I don't look it and I beat my 37 year old male friend in an ultra marathon 😜

Now she is qualifying herself.

So that's why I wrote 38 on my profile

Ooh, deceitful! It's really not a problem, I can see that you're the kinda person who just wants to live it. I'm into that.

Time to relate.

I promise I won't cripple you. ; )

Time to joke.

I see what you mean, 37 is more believable than 44.

07 ICE ICE

She gave me her number, the comfort was successful.

# Tinder: Are These Really The Best Photos You Have Of Yourself?

So ask yourself. *'Are these really the best photos I have of myself?'*

Over the course of a few years, I have seen guys post their Tinder profiles, showing their pictures and asking f or advice or potential improvements. Most guys always fail at one thing; missing the point. Some guys put up photos of themselves from 20 years earlier when they were a kid. What is the point of that? Nobody is going to care about your childhood, these girls did not go on Tinder to date people based on photos of children. Whatever you show on Tinder needs to be time-relevant; your present self. If you look different from a photo from long ago, do not post it.

Some guys also put up photos of themselves in a crowd or surrounded by friends. If you were swiping through Tinder right now and you saw a photo of 5 girls but you did not know which one is the girl, you would not exactly take your chances on that if you were to go on a date without the information of which one she is, unless they are all attractive to you. If you are seeing someone's profile and it is not immediately clear who's profile it is, you should not bother. So why would a girl do the same if all of your photos are just bro photos? If you ever put up a photo of you with other people, the best of the best of a group photo is one in which you are the center of attention. If that is not the case, then either the attention is focused on someone or something else or it is just seemingly an equal photo of some friends. If you have a photo where you are the center of attention, it will inspire subconscious thoughts to those who see. Who is this guy? What does he do? Why is he so popular? Why does everyone like him? There are endless possible thoughts that draw in positive assumptions just from a   photo. If you want the best, you have to put in the best. If you don't have such a photo, make one.

I have also witnessed profiles that consist of nothing but selfies or pictures of oneself without anything else going on. Are you really that bored? Is there nothing exciting in your life?

### Someone's Profile

There is far too much 'bro' here.

The first photo is touristic and a side shot, so it doesn't show the face very well. The third photo is literally where Hitler stood for the same photo. Every photo after that involves too much 'bro' and it is not personal enough. The final photo isn't even a photo of the guy, it's just a stupid meme.

### Someone's Profile

The photo of the guitar would be the strongest by far. The fourth photo does not even show the guy in the photo, The fifth photo may be a good general photo, but it is possibly too zoomed out. The final photo may also be to zoomed out.

## Someone's Profile

I met this guy. We live in the same city, and in fact his second photo was taken at the club I used to go to every single week.

Anyway, when Ben showed me his profile he mentioned that he has had a lot of success with it, and the first 3 photos he has really help that. His first photo is relaxed and has a nice atmosphere. His second photo is of him holding a blonde girl, and the girl is super happy but his face is neutrally mischievous, which not only makes it look fun but also shows the social proof that there is a girl that is super happy in his effect. This third photo is peaceful, scenic and looks great. The last 3 though are more 'bro' photos and not as good, and he still has room for 3 more photos to reach the limit of 9 photos.

His bio is also extremely well made. It is simple. Everyone loves garlic bread. Most things he says in the bio are very lighthearted and humorous; it makes you picture things in your mind which makes it very effective. You're already imagining playing hide and seek in IKEA.

## Ben 23

The Manchester Metropolitan University

less than a kilometre away

Garlic bread enthusiast.

Can cook minuite rice in 57 seconds.

Unbeaten Monopoly champion since 2007.

Looking for someone to play hide and seek inside IKEA with Or go to Legoland with.

**Someone's Profile**

This guy was already doing well on Tinder. His photos are great. His third photo is of him and his dog, and for this type of photo it really couldn't get much better than that.

You can see his positivity and his style.

**Someone's Profile**

This guy from Texas s hared his profile and said he already gets quite a lot of success with it. Some of the reasons behind this are that it's very simple and focuses on him. It is not trying too hard and it shows a good range of emotions.

### Ice's Profile

This is my own profile. It has been through so many changes in the space of 2 years. Photo 1 shows a powerful pose by a beach with a long beard, this was placed as the main photo because I noticed it gained a lot of likes on Facebook; so there was already evidence that it was a good photo. Photo 2 used to be the main photo, it shows me in a suit sitting while a girl has her legs on me and she is wearing platform high h eels. This was modelling. Photo 4 shows social proof and preselection so that girls can see I am capable of hanging out with hot girls. Photo 6 is a photo of myself and a club promoter on stage with a DJ in the background and thousands of people partying behind us. Photo 7 is just a photo of me on an AirBNB bed surrounded by cats.

High quality photos are important.

# Tinder Assignment

So, are they *really* your best photos?

If the answer is yes, you can do better.

If the answer is no, not only can you create better photos, but you already have better photos. So use the best of what you already have, but be on a mission actively to create more. Be an opportunist. Do fun things and capture it.

Your assignment is to create and collect better photos of yourself from this very moment, and this assignment will expire when you die. This is your lifelong commitment. It is your life mission to be an opportunist when it comes to photo opportunities. This could mean the difference between you matching with that girl on Tinder, or never meeting. This could be the difference between meeting someone really important, or missing the opportunity and never knowing it. You have so much to gain.

If you do not have a good enough camera, buy one or borrow one. Find a friend or a photographer to help you out. Even a small amount of practice will improve your arsenal of photos in the present and future. Even use your phone. The perfect phone for this is any Google Pixel; it has unlimited photo and video storage and extremely good camera technology.

On Tinder you will be judged immediately based on your photos. It is therefore important to think about how your photos can be the best they can possibly be. For example, if you would like to use a group photo or take a group photo, make sure that you are dominating the photo and that you are the subject; everyone there must be at your effect and you must be the cause. Visualize a group photo with three people; you must ideally be in the middle and it should look like the other two are happy because of you. Some people have massive group photos of perhaps 10 or more people. Don't make it hard for people to find you in a photo, it must be immediately obvious and about you. A photo of 10 people is most likely not a photo about you, it is a photo about the group.

Some people put up photos of pets. It is better to have a photo of you holding the pet than a photo of just the pet; you're not selling the dog on eBay, you're supposed to be marketing your personal image of your physical body to girls. Every photo must have you in it, and it must also be clear and big enough to see you.

If your entire profile just consists of selfies, give this book to a friend and tell them to throw it at your head. Selfies are not ideal. If you have a mirror selfie, that's far worse and I would not like to be responsible for the damage inflicted upon you, but someone has to teach you a lesson. Don't ever do mirror selfies.

# Snapchat: Is It Worth It?

In early 2018 Snapchat had an update that saw a completely new design. It was not popular, and as a result, Snapchat lost some popularity. It is still prominent, but it is far less important than Instagram or Facebook. However, for the sake of variety, I will include some of my experiences from Snapchat.

I personally do not like Snapchat anymore and do not even use it anymore, and this was because of the unpopular 2018 update. Regardless of what we think about the update, it needs to be very clear that Snapchat is useless when it comes to building an audience or having something public; everything disappears in a matter of hours. Are you really going to check Snapchat every single day for the rest of your life? This question is precisely why you should invest into Instagram and Facebook significantly more than Snapchat. If you already use Snapchat a lot, you are probably missing out on even bigger potential on Instagram and Facebook.

In addition, let's face it; Snapchat is for 13 year olds anyway.

Instagram and Facebook bring things to the table that Snapchat does not: a timeline, a profile, and a sense of long-term lasting. Snapchat is far too focused on the present, and that is its ultimate downfall. If it lacks a past, it won't have much of a future.

| OPTIONS & DETAILS BELOW | | | |
|---|---|---|---|
| Messaging | ✓ | ✓ | ✓ |
| Stories | ✓ | ✓ | ✓ |
| Timeline | X | ✓ | ✓ |
| Short Term | ✓ | ✓ | ✓ |
| Long Term | X | ✓ | ✓ |
| Fans | ✓ | ✓ | ✓ |
| Friends | X | X | ✓ |

| | |
|---|---|
| 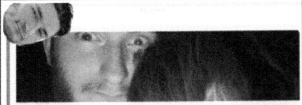<br>What do we have here.. yet again a different girl<br><br>ME<br>No, no. She dyed her hair again. | **Snapchat**<br><br>A girl responding to my story. |
| <br>You are literally with a different girl every day<br><br>ME<br>It's the same one each time, I promise. She dyes her hair and bleaches her skin a lot.<br>Shh. | **Snapchat**<br><br>Responding to my story again. |
| <br>True.<br><br>ME<br>Come. So I can drown you. 😼<br><br>You're a bitch<br><br>I'll come<br>AH WAIT drown me in your semen pls | **Snapchat**<br><br>Another girl responded to my story.<br><br><br><br>She escalates it sexually. |

Your snaps enter
I*entertain
*entertain me
Fucked that up
Anyway
*your snaps are entertaining

ME
I know. Lots of fun. I wank over them every night too.

Same

ME
Perfect. You need to come party so we can syncronize.

Don't think you'll be able to keep up

ME
Let's see about that. Monday.

Have this instead

Hahahahahah
You saved it

**Snapchat**

She likes my stories.

I take the piss out of it.

Planting an idea related to meeting.

Planning to meet.

She sends nudes.

| | |
|---|---|
| **ME**<br>Mmm, I like it.<br><br>I save literally everything. I hate that I gotta save each line of messages.<br><br>Setting it as my background on my desktop and everything. ; )<br><br><br>Hahanah are you actually?<br><br>**ME**<br>Just kidding. Maybe it should be your new contact picture if you feel you're naughty enough for that.<br><br>Go for it haha | Shamelessly saved the photo.<br><br><br><br>Joking with her.<br><br><br><br><br><br>We had sex but shortly after that she got engaged and moved away. |
| Hey google man ! Next Monday I'll be back in London for 4 days !<br><br>**ME**<br>♥<br><br>I'm mostly available on Monday and Thursday, madame.<br><br>**ICE**<br>Let see on Thursday !<br><br>**ME**<br>Beautiful, gimme three ideas of things you wanna do. ⚡<br><br>**ICE**<br>Winter wonderland for sure !<br>But after I don't have any idea<br><br>**ME**<br>Good call, I need to go there. Let's do it.<br>Do you have WhatsApp?<br><br>**ICE**<br>Yeah :) <br> | **Snapchat**<br><br>The advantage is having the interactive map, knowing where people are. She is coming to my city from another country and wants to meet.<br><br><br><br><br><br><br><br><br><br>Something fun to do.<br><br><br>Phone number, because why not? |

Reminds me of you.

**ICE E**
Aha how so

ME
She's **ICE** and almost as weird as you.

**ICE ICE**
I love this
No I'm not that weird... z

ME
Just crazy. ; )

**ICE**
Well meh

**ICE ICE**
Are you really in Holland atm

ME
Y ; )
Where you at?

**ICE ICE**
I'm in London
At my new office
Would love for you to come by

**Snapchat**

I sent a girl a video of me and another girl messing around.

Simple stuff.

I show her a photo.

Blah blah blah.

Asks me a question, so she wants to continue the conversation.

She wants me to visit her.

| | |
|---|---|
| **ME**<br>I'm gonna be gone for the weekend, but send me the details. Maybe I can visit on Monday. ; )<br><br>**ICE ICE**<br>Fantastic!<br><br>How about in my boardroom<br><br>**ME**<br>How about everywhere?<br><br>**ICE ICE**<br>Sure<br><br>Boardroom first<br><br>I would like to make the guys jealous<br><br>**ME**<br>Maybe we should film it. All about them angles.<br><br>**ICE ICE**<br>Yes it is now a days<br><br>Can google use it as a homepage thing<br><br>**ME**<br>We can use it as whatever we want.<br><br>**ICE ICE**<br>Fantastic!<br><br>I'll book the boardroom for a solid 3 hours Monday morning<br><br>**ME**<br>Good. Where is it?<br><br>**ICE ICE**<br>**ICE** street<br><br>**ME**<br>Not far from where I work a lot of the time. ; ) | I can visit her soon.<br><br><br><br>She wants to have sex with me in her office.<br><br><br><br><br><br><br><br><br><br><br><br><br><br><br><br><br><br><br><br>Interesting. |

# Understanding Message Game in Depth

Following the original Message Game Guide (2018) that was made before this book, there were some quite useful insights from followers.

The original Message Game Guide (2018), released in February 2018, spawned a very loyal and active following on Telegram. If you would like to join it, find the Message Game group on Facebook. Message Game is more than just a guide, it is a lifestyle. It is a way of life, it is a way to achieve things and a w ay to succeed in dating. In order to maximize your dating potential, it will be very useful to join the rest of those who also read this. Get involved, dive straight in and it will prove to be very valuable to your life.

### Facebook Group
Ice White's Message Game
Facebook.com/groups/MessageGame

### Telegram Group
Message Game
(See Facebook Group)

### Instagram
IceWhiteOfficial

### Facebook
Ice White

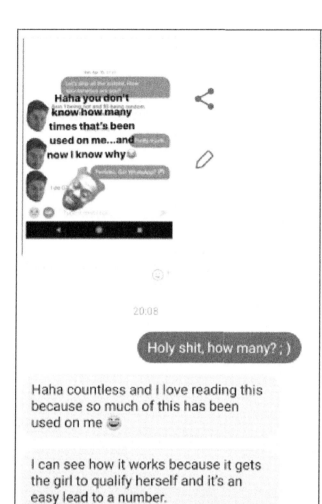

Haha countless and I love reading this because so much of this has been used on me 😄

I can see how it works because it gets the girl to qualify herself and it's an easy lead to a number.
But I never replied to those because I just thought "why is he so entitled? 1 qualifier isn't enough to take me out. Plus I'm not really reaction seeing.

## Female Message Game Follower

A female that joined the Message Game community realized that she had received messages inspired by the original Message Game Guide (2018). She sent to me:

*Haha you don't know how many times that's been used on me...and now I know why*

She rightly stated that the original and classic Message Game line, regarding spontaneity, brings girls to qualify themselves. She claims to have never fallen for it, but she has fallen for Message Game.

To summarize, Message Game will always win. We will always find a way, and it will come get you.

summary of fundamentals I noticed observing this chat

- Don't send shit that doesn't give ANY value to the conversation
- Either your conversation is heading somewhere or you're being a **boring useless needy prick**
- Aim to set a date after a spike in emotions or something like that, overall just **don't be a bitch and set a date**, be very specific about the **details**, you're the dude that plans it all out, don't leave her any room to think about it
- If she says no you don't care because you have **abundance**, she might even see that and hit you up later
- My personal opinion but emojis are **so gay** oh my god please stop sending crying laughing emojis unless something truly is hilarious
- Overall keep things short, precise, to the point, don't waste time on chit-chat and **GET TO THE POINT**, you'll have fun with her when you see eachother bro
- **Be spontaneous in answering**, are you a busy dude working on your mission in life? Well if not what are you doing mate, fix that shit and your text game / game overall will explode

- Have fun, self-amuse, don't take this shit seriously

11:43

**Message Game Summary**

A follower wrote up his observations from the thinking that is surrounding Message Game.

He summarized it very well, so this is a very valuable summary from a follower's perspective.

Hey Ice, following up on your text game. I get stuck between whether to text her often or only specifically to meet up. I know there's a balance which I've been doing but my main question is after you meet up with the girl would you text her daily or keep it minimal again till you meet up.
19:35

Call it message game from now. We are fucking rebranding and reinventing this shit.
20:50

Stop being a whiny bitch validating yourself by wanting attention from girls all the time.
20:50

I just had a date with a girl today, but I didn't respond to her message from two days ago. We have had no contact, but still made it happen. Why?

Because I knew I didn't need to respond.
20:51

I don't message anyone daily. 20:51

Force yourself into abundance, stop relying on one girl or a few girls.
20:52

If a girl messages me about something, I will follow that but also aim it to something.

If I am messaging anyone in any case, it is aimed at a result. Not to validate myself. To have an outcome. NECESSITY ONLY. 20:53

It makes sense 🙍 I tend to always have the "abundance" mentality but that just opened up a wider horizon.
20:57

Aiming it to something is the main reason why I have been able to get dates with your text game so I 100% agree on that too.
20:59

When you don't have loads of girls that you're talking to I can see clearly how me I have fallen into that validation trap.
21:01

I didn't message a girl for one week and got a date the next day 🌱 whereas I would message a girl daily and not even get a date.
21:02

Thanks for the info bro 21:04

## Message Daily Or Message Necessarily

A fair question.

To give you a feel for how my day-to-day life should be, I do not message anyone daily. What is the point?

Necessity only is the answer. You have a goal, and you must try to achieve it. There are only two possible outcomes of message game - meeting or not meeting.

If you prefer not to meet, you are wasting your time.

If you want to meet but you are not trying to make it happen, you are wasting your time.

## Female Tinder Profile Experiment

A Tinder profile was made using the photos of a female Message Game follower. Within 5 minutes of the account existing, more than 100 male profiles swiped right on the profile.

To put that into perspective, most guys struggle to reach 100 matches, and most never get more than 300 in total even if they have used it for years. If it takes a man a year to reach 100 matches and a woman 5 minutes to reach 100 matches, is there a problem with the balance?

Yes. This photo was taken after 24 hours of the profile existing. It reached 2,326 right swipes that had not yet been matched. There were already 45 matches, which then actually means that 2,371 male profiles swiped right in the first 24 hours.

99% of male profiles will never get this many right swipes in their lifetime.

To some people, this may be really scary. It is. This is why Message Game is important, it will give you the chance to come out on top and give you more chances than most guys will ever have.

Unless they see tremendeous value in what you offer you might consider following-up with their communication. What you might be trying is to close the deal from advertising alone, they saw your profile and that's all they got, still, what's in it for them?

@IceWhiteOfficial does wonders with the "name 3 things..." question, it's both a screen and a signal for them to invest time, thought and their imagination along with opening up a bit which gives him the information he can use to follow-up the conversation.

You've seen how even when his texts are "biblicly" long they remain relevant and in-line with the topic, appearing non-needy and genuinly interesting.

## Behind The Message Itself

An active member of the Message Game Telegram group responded to a guy who was asking for some advice.

Be relevant. Be non-needy. Be interesting.

# Ice Game

I have a list to share with you that are great date ideas. I personally do not like to meet people just for drinks or for coffee because I find these very boring; I don't even like coffee or tea.

These suggestions include some of my favorites and I personally love food so it may be a little biased in that sense; however you just need to be aware that not everything listed is suitable for everyone, and not everything you see will even be your style. Have some awareness. For example, classy girls may not want to have some greasy American food or may not want to go to a buffet. Girls really dedicated to fitness may not want to involve themselves with pizza, waffles and milkshakes. Vegans or vegetarians may not appreciate a BBQ that involves nothing but meat. Think about what kind of girl she is and what she would find most appealing. To find out, you just need to learn a bit more about her or put a few suggestions to her.

| Places To Eat/Drink | Home |
|---|---|
| Brunch | Baking |
| Buffet | BBQ |
| Chinese Food | Blanket Fort |
| Dessert | Cooking |
| Hot Chocolates | Massaging |
| Ice Cream | Movies |
| Japanese Food | Netflix |
| Mexican Food | Pancakes |
| Milkshakes | Pillow Fights |
| Pancakes | Pillow Fort |
| Pizza | Predrinks |
| Street Food | Trampoline |
| Tacos | Waffles |
| Vietnamese Food | |
| Waffles | |
| **Standard** | **Adventure** |
| Bowling | Axe Throwing |
| Comedy Show | Beach |
| Golf (Mini/Crazy/Driving Range) | Boat Trip |
| Markets | Escape Room |
| Movie Theater | Feeding Animals |
| Museum | IKEA |
| Park | Skating |
| Party | Skydiving |
| Picnic | Speakeasy |
| Shopping | Trampolining |
| Walking | Wind Tunnels |

You should also be aware that the Home and Adventure categories are often less practical or require more comfort and trust between you and the girl. For example, she may be scared of heights and would therefore be more inclined to say no to skydiving. In addition to that, not everyone has a place to skydive near them, and not every location has places like axe throwing, or boat trips. In terms of the Home suggestions, not every girl is comfortable in the idea of going to your house or apartment when you only just met.

Let's redefine what a **date** is. A date is when you meet a girl, by arranging to meet, to do something together with the purpose of potentially building some form of relationship. That relationship could be mainly casual sex, or that relationship could be a more classical long-term relationship leading to marriage. Ultimately, at the very least, you are friends. If you choose to meet as friends, that's okay. It has the potential to become more than friends, therefore it's important to still think of it as a date. If you interact with a female using a **friend frame,** there will be no expectations like those labelled onto the classic **dating frame.** I believe it is better to build a relationship with someone without expectations than to build a relationship with someone by having expectations. If you are expecting the other person to kiss you, pay the bill or anything else, then your expectation will either be fulfilled or not be fulfilled, which therefore means it can fail. If you have no expectations for the other person because you are just treating each other like friends, you have nothing to worry about because friendships do not ever truly fail. Friends can either be friends or become more than friends. The friend frame is informal, and the dating frame is formal.

Dating Frame:
1. Has higher expectations
2. Can easily lead to the princess mentality problem
3. Is a lot more serious and formal
4. You can only continue dating or never see each other again
5. There is very little potential to grow beyond dating
6. There is a lot of potential for the relationship to collapse

Friend Frame:
1. Has lower expectations
2. Is far more equal
3. Is far more casual and informal
4. You can, at the very least, be friends forever
5. There is a lot of potential for the relationship to grow beyond friends 6. There is very little potential for the relationship to collapse

This is not to say that you should be using Tinder or dating to make friends, it is to say that it is better to come from more of a friend frame than from a dating one. The point of dating is to find sexual partners, either to be *just* a sexual partner or to be a sexual partner that will be your long term best friend. Following this logic, it should be better to come from a frame that sees you and who you may be dating as best friends, not two people interviewing each other for two job roles or life roles. Having an informal relationship is best.

Now let's redefine game.

**Primary game** is how you physically meet people. Primary game is in the present; meeting people now.

| Primary Game | | | |
|---|---|---|---|
| Cold Approach | | Social Circle Game | |
| Day Game | Night Game | Club Game | Social Media Game |

Most people in the seduction community subscribe primarily to cold approach methods, while some people subscribe primarily to social circle game.

Within cold approach, there is day game and night game. Day gamers like to go out on the streets to meet people, or even in shopping malls and parks or other places during the day where people like to g o and exist. Night gamers like to go out at night and meet people in bars, clubs and sometimes streets too.

Within social circle game, there is club game and social media game as the two main components. Club game is where night gamers and social circle gamers shake hands. They both like clubs. However, social circle gamers use clubs f or preselection and social proof; they will tend to go to the club with girls who are already with them, whereas night gamers will tend to enter without girls and find girls inside. Social circle gamers also like using social media to meet people; so they may f or example have a relatively high value profile on Instagram and be able to get girls to meet them by using social media; a component of message game.

When meeting people through primary game, I have two useful ways of optimal closing.

## How to Facebook-close:

1.  Tell her to get her phone out.
2.  Use her phone to send yourself a friend request.

Facebook-closing this way is the optimal way. Once you send yourself a friend request, the ball is in your court and you won't be dependent on her accepting if you did things the opposite way by using your phone to send her a friend request.

## How to number-close:

1.  Tell her to get her phone out.
2.  Put your name and number into her contacts.
3.  Send yourself a stupid message.

Number-closing this way means that it's more fun and you know it's the right phone number because it's your number added to her phone. Plus, you already have a message from her, that you sent, that you can respond to at a convenient time for you.

**Secondary game** is how you remain connecting to people you have either met or not yet met, in order to communicate and meet in the future. Message game is in the future; meeting people in the future.

| Secondary Game | | |
| --- | --- | --- |
| Message Game | | |
| Messaging | Online Dating | Social Media Game |

Message game is a secondary game concept. No matter which primary game mode you subscribe to and use, your secondary game will always be message game. If you meet someone on a street and intend to meet again, you will exchange details. If you meet someone at a club and want to meet again, you will exchange details. If you meet someone on a train, a bus, a plane, a gym, or any place where you cannot guarantee you will easily find this person again, you will exchange details if you want to meet again. Every path of primary game; both cold approach and social circle game, will lead you to message game. You can use messaging one on one just like through SMS, you can use online dating like Tinder; you can also use social media to your advantage. These are the three types of message game; you can use any of them and as many of them as you want. Some people do not like social media, so would prefer to use the other two. Some people do not like online dating so may use the other two, or just one other.

Every single person needs message game unless they live in a forest without electricity. Message game is relevant to all other forms of game.

# The End

Everything seen here has been collected between late 2016 and mid 2019. If that is the span of two and a half years; of which the first year was not even developed into any kind of theory or system, then imagine the future. In this time, I have dated many amazing people. I dated models. I had sex with dozens of girls in such short time and built relationships that are more meaningful in addition to that. I travelled thousands of miles with girls I had magical connections with. I had cozy nights in watching many movies and TV shows from *The Mummy* to *How I Met Your Mother*. I had many adventures from mountain climbing to going backstage at concerts every week and being invited to comedy shows. I ate at all kinds of places, from the world's best poutinerie in Montréal to the greasiest chicken and waffles in London. I was treated. I had girls take me out for surprises. I had girls buy me food out of their own will. I hosted photoshoots. Girls even came to me for photoshoots and I'm not even a photographer. I had great times. However, most importantly, if all of this happened in the space of two years… Think about what the rest of your life could be like from now on. Life changing, right? You may have another 40-50 years left to live. You have time, and plenty of it. Have patience, but remember that you are already on your way. Now you have everything you need.

If this has helped you in any way, I want you to give me a token of appreciation back by following me on Instagram, Facebook or YouTube if not already.

If what you learned in this book contributed to your relationship with someone, I want you to be grateful for every moment and be happy with that person.

If you ever marry someone because of this book, invite me to your wedding. I will be there and I will sing for you.

If you ever have children because of this book, name them after me or something. Whatever you find fitting.

It is now your job to get out there and meet people. Have adventures, do amazing things, and communicate effectively. You now have more control over what happens next. Use it to your advantage. The rest of your journey is up to you.

The only way is up.

**Facebook**

Facebook.com/IceWhiteOfficial

**Instagram**

@IceWhiteOfficial

Books, teachings and people that inspired the methodology of Message Game are the following:

1. Ockham's Razor - William Of Ockham (1300s)

   *Ockham's razor is the concept around simplicity; particularly in that the simplest explanations and solutions are often the greatest.*

2. The Art Of War - Sun Tzu (400s)

   *'If you know the enemy and know yourself, you need not fear the result of a hundred battles. If you know yourself but not the enemy, for every victory gained you will also suffer a defeat. If you know neither the enemy nor yourself, you will succumb in every battle.'*

3. The Game - Neil Strauss (2005)

   *The Message Game is a response to the evolution of the community mentioned within Neil Strauss's book, and how the community has evolved since 2002 in order to adapt to technological changes that makes Message Game far more important than any other aspect mentioned in or formed because of 'The Game'.*

Big thank you to the thousands of people who read the original Message Game Guide (2018) on Google Docs from the beginning of 2018 until the release of this book. Thank you to the many hundreds of people who gave feedback and joined the groups before a book was even in consideration. Shout out to the many great supporters from Dallas, Austin, Chicago, New York, Toronto, Ottawa, London, Moscow and the many other random places one may not expect.

**Artwork & Illustration**

Alyona Ermolina (Abend Nebel)
ArtStation.com/abendnebel
abendnebel11@gmail.com

# Glossary

Terms marked with * are recommended to research further in order to understand more due to the complex nature of their context and usage; these phrases are quite often misunderstood.

**Bullshit:** In message game terms, anything you say that does not take a step towards meeting a girl is called *bullshit*. Comfort would not be *bullshit*, but small talk would. Example; when you message a girl asking how she is or when you talk to her about anything without a purpose of meeting. Coined by Ice White.

**Date:** An activity with a girl, or with multiple girls, who you are interested in. It has the potential to host the start of a physical romance.

**Dating frame:** Setting your relationship with someone as formal as if you are on a first date and getting to know each other. Example; when you go out on a date, talk about yourself to each other, and ask each other questions.

**DHV:** *Demonstration of higher value*; your perceived value is increased through demonstration of a skill or attribute. Example; having many Instagram followers.

**Flake:** When a girl cancels a date or does not show up.

**Frame*:** How something is perceived. Coined by Richard Bandler and John Grinder.

**Friend frame:** Setting your relationship with someone as informal from the beginning as if you were friends in order to bypass the unnecessary bullshit that comes with the dating frame. Example; when you hang out with a girl as friends instead of coming from a dating frame so that your interaction and time together is less serious and has no expectations. Coined by Ice White.

**Fuckbuddy:** A person that you have sex with casually without emotional or long-term expectations.

**Game:** The ability to influence behaviors or people in a particular way in order to create some kind of relationship. Example; when you go out to meet and game girls to set up a date so that your mom could stop telling you to get a girlfriend.

**Hot girl reality:** The uniqueness of how a girl behaves based on how people treat her because of many males being attracted towards her and acting in a certain way that has validated her ego to make her f eel as if she is extremely attractive. Example; when everybody wants to fuck a particular girl. Coined by Ice White.

**IOI\*:** *Indicator of interest*; a sign that a woman gives a man that indirectly reveals some extent of interest or attraction towards him, whether or not the sign is extremely subtle. Example; when she re-initiates the conversation when you stop talking; when she asks what your name is; when she plays with her hair when she looks at you. Coined by Erik Von Markovik.

**Kino\*:** *Kinesthesia*; touching or being touched with intent or purpose of arousal or to proceed to further sexual contact. Example; when you hold her hands; when you stroke her hair, when you hold her hips or shoulders. Coined by Ross Jeffries.

**Logistics:** The level of ease of transportation. Example; if you live Downtown you have really good logistics to bring a girl home from a date, you have bad logistics if you are on a date and your place is far away or not easy to get to.

**Number-close:** Acquiring a woman's phone number. Coined by Erik Von Markovik.

**Onto the next:** When an interaction with a girl isn't going anywhere at the present time, try interacting with a few other girls before coming back to the original said girl.

**Opener:** Something said to initiate a conversation. Example; *'hello', 'let's skip all the bullshit, how spontaneous are you?'*

**Pimpspiration:** Inspiration in the form of a man's success with women. Coined by Ice White.

**Preselection:** The idea that women are attracted to men who already attract other women, showing that a particular man is already approved or proven to be accepted by women. Example; when you have a photoshoot with hot girls and upload the photos to Instagram, resulting in girls finding you more attractive because you were able to do this.

**Princess mentality:** The behavior of a woman who has one-sided expectations whereby she wishes to be given more in a relationship than what she can or will contribute. Example; when a woman expects a man to pay for the bill and to pay for her taxi. Coined by Ice White.

**Screening:** Assessing someone based on his or her suitability for something. Example; *'how adventurous are you?'; 'how far away do you live?'*

**Sexual frustration:** The frustration caused by a lack of satisfaction in someone's sexual activity. Example; when you are sexually frustrated because you are a 40-year-old virgin or you are having a dry spell.

**Shit test\*:** Something that a woman has said to a man that will, based on his response, give her information on whether or not he is strong enough to be worthy of being a boyfriend or sexual partner. If he takes her words literally or too seriously, he will fail the test and lose the opportunity to proceed in their potential relationship. You should take a shit test as an IOI, because it opens up the opportunity to pass a test that others will fail. It is ultimately a frame test. Example; *'you are too young for me'; 'you probably say that to all the girls'; 'is that your pickup line?'*

**Simplify:** The idea that everything in message game is easier when it is the least complex it could be, inspired by the philosophy behind Ockham's razor. Coined by Ice White.

**Social proof:** The psychosocial phenomenon whereby people perceive someone by their already-achieved social status or influence. Example; when you have many photos of yourself with different girls; when you have over a million followers on Instagram. Coined by Robert Cialdini.

**Tall guy theory:** A metaphor in relation to the *hot girl reality* to explain that very tall people often hear the same old remarks from people they meet. Example; *'wow, you are so tall'; 'what is the weather like up there?', 'you could get something off the top shelf for me.'* Coined by Ice White.

**Validation:** Gaining approval, whether by seeking it or unintentionally receiving it, which boosts the ego and provides the dopamine effect. Example; when a girl wants you to follow her on Instagram just to get likes and followers; when your profile picture on Facebook gets many likes.

**Wife material:**  A woman who you would consider a great life-partner and candidate for marriage. Example; when a girl is very cute and loyal and also doesn't post pictures solely of her ass on Instagram; when a girl truly cares about you and will go to great lengths for you and your relationship.

# Situation Index

If the girl is behaving a certain way, this page lists pages where there are examples.

| Situation | Chapters |
|---|---|
| She is ignoring me/she isn't very responsive | 17, 64-67, 93, 122, 128-129, 132-133, 134, 142, 156, 163, 164, 165, 166-170, 170, 171, 176, 182, 185-186 |
| She is giving me a shit test | 64-67, 78, 89, 92, 107, 121, 166-170, 180 |
| She says she is busy | 28-30, 52, 62, 64, 113, 132, 137, 154, 171, 174, 181-182 |
| She only wants to meet for coffee or drinks | 61 |
| She is only visiting my city/town | 28-30, 54-55, 79, 140, 176, 201 |
| Logistics are bad | 28-30, 31-32, 49, 64-67, 80, 140, 141, 161-162, 172-173 |
| She thinks I just want sex | 54, 56-57, 73, 78, 81-82, 90, 107, 108, 140, 145-146, 165, 177 |
| Phone calls | 6, 22, 177 |
| She wants more out of the relationship | 11, 90, 109-110, 145-146, 148, 161-162, 179, 180, 187 |
| She wants to use me to get something | 24, 147, 166-170 |
| She gave me the wrong number or details | 136 |
| Inviting multiple girls to a date | 63, 174 |
| Spontaneous line | 4, 17, 47, 48, 74, 77, 92, 93, 94, 95, 96, 97, 98, 99, 100, 101, 102, 103, 104, 105, 106, 107, 108, 111, 114, 115, 116, 120, 121, 122, 124, 127, 130, 131, 134, 170, 175, 205 |
| Adventurous line | 11, 17, 19, 20, 21, 27, 47, 48, 53, 56, 60, 62, 68, 72, 76, 81, 85, 117, 123, 136, 137, 150, 163, 165, 166, 171, 185, 188 |
| 3 things line | 11, 27, 49, 60, 62, 68, 96, 114, 116, 117, 120, 122, 124, 120, 131, 150, 171, 188, 209 |

# Frequently Asked Questions

An extremely simplified version of questions and answers.

### How long should I wait to reply to her?

The time it takes you to reply should be longer than the time it took her to reply, or long enough to demonstrate that you're not just some sucker who is waiting around all day for her to give you attention. Of course, if she took a year to reply, don't copy that. In such extreme cases, generally wait a few days or a week if it is time pressing.

### Do I need to talk to her every day?

No. Stop. What the fuck are you doing? Message her to meet. Don't be pen pals. You only need to start messaging her if you want to meet her, and you need to get to meeting her as quickly and efficiently as possible.

### What if she cannot meet me or is too busy to meet me until two weeks from now?

Don't try to keep it warm. Don't try to keep the conversation going, you will run out of things to talk about and you will also be talking without purpose other than only to fill the time. Ask her when approximately she will be less busy, if she says she will be busy for two weeks, tell her you will check in on her in two weeks. Then do exactly that. Don't interact with her for two weeks, then go back into the conversation and arrange to meet her.

### What if a girl I matched with on Tinder has not responded to my opener?

If you sent her a message and got absolutely nothing back, don't try to reinitiate unless it is over 20 days since you tried to open her. You don't even know her and she doesn't even know you, so don't be desperate for the attention of a girl who has never even messaged you. Send her a GIF, not words. The GIF would at least show up on her messages page as a GIF, and for her to see it she will have to look at the message itself.

### Should I use superlikes on Tinder?

Yes. Only use it on girls you are genuinely interested in, and try not to superlike girls just because they are hot; other guys are doing the same. Superlikes work best with girls who are really new to Tinder that have not yet met anyone.

### What if she is being mean to me?

Grow up and have some balls. You should have standards, and you should also not be offended by anyone, especially by a girl you have never even met or hardly know. If you react, you're no better than a baby. Don't fall into her frame.

**What if she says she has a boyfriend or says she isn't looking for a relationship?**

Make it clear that you're not looking to get into a relationship. Just be honest. Via the friend frame, you can meet. However, that doesn't mean that you will just be friends when you meet her, it means you can take that relationship to a higher level and form a sexual relationship. All she needs to know is that you're seemingly just friends, and you will be exactly that, but with potential benefits.

**How do I create attraction?**

Attraction is in your behavior and how your profiles are set up. You already created it, just improve your behaviors and profiles. She will be attracted to the behaviors laid out in this book about being non-needy, abundant, honest and simple. Your decisiveness, good communication and bullshit skipping should also demonstrate attractiveness automatically for you.

**What will happen if your techniques become outdated?**

Then join the Message Game group on Facebook for any updated or new content and methods. It is likely that dating apps and communication methods will change in the next 10, 20 and 50 years; however, the principles will remain the same. After all, you are far more likely to get a girl on a date if you talk about date ideas and then going for it, than to talk about random things, building up a conversation and building up the confidence to ask her out; the latter wastes too much time. If 9 out of 10 guys are trying to 'build attraction' and conversations with a particular girl and that one other guy is getting to the point and asking her out, it's obvious who will get further.

**Should I swipe right on Tinder for all girls?**

No. Swipe only on girls you feel you can get along with that are also relatively attractive to you. If you match with a fat woman on Tinder and you are not into fat women, then you're not going to do anything with it anyway. Don't ruin your position in the algorithm by telling it that you have no standards. You need to have standards.

**What if I want to action a Facebook-close but she doesn't have Facebook?**

Then that's something you have to ask her. What does she have? Use your initiative.

**Should you tailor your method around a girl's perceived personality, or go with the same method for every girl?**

Stick with a particular method for most cases. If you feel that you will get on extremely well with someone in particular, then there is less to worry about if you tailor your approach to suit a different path. If you tailor your messaging for every single girl, you're wasting a lot of mental energy trying to adapt to everyone's differing personalities, and it is definitely wasting a lot of time if you do not manage to get anyone on dates fast.

**If I haven't built a good Instagram or Facebook profile yet, what should I do in the meantime?**

You have to start from somewhere. This is a long-term game. Build it up over time; it is better to add little by little over time than to do absolutely nothing and miss out on opportunities and potential down the line. You can start now and in 2-5 years, it could be epic. The only way is up.

**How can I maintain interest and attraction up until the date?**

In the simplest terms, it should be attractive enough of you to be the guy who gets things done by arranging a date that is fun that she will look forward to. What you shouldn't do is waste the time between the arrangement of the date and the date itself on talking about things you could have left for the date itself. Do not get to know each other until then, and keep the messaging minimal. You already have the date set; you don't need to achieve much else. However, hours or a day before the date you should send something relevant to the upcoming date. For example *'What will you be wearing?'* is good to check that the date will still happen without asking if the date will still happen. *'Look for the tall skinny white guy wearing blue jeans and a white shirt carrying an ice cream cone'* is good to send 1-5 hours before the date to make it easy for her to find you, as well as show her that you communicate well enough for her to have no worries. Obviously, if you're not tall, skinny, white, wearing blue jeans and a white shirt or carrying an ice cream cone, write something else.

### How should I escalate when it comes to the date itself?

This book has given you the guide to get the date, but it is not one about making the date successful. That, my friend, is up to you now. However, I will share one tremendous tip of mine that is so simple and easily forgotten that it makes people cry in regret that they didn't do this. Hold her hand. You can do it while walking, while dancing, just about anywhere. All you need is a hand of your own and a hand of hers. Remember when holding hands was so innocent when you were a kid? It still is. Your first step of escalating should be holding hands. Many people mistake kissing for being first. Just hold her hand. If she asks why you are doing it, just say you felt like it. If she pulls her hand away, then she's not ready for anything yet. If she accepts it, as most girls do under the right circumstances of game, you are doing good.

Printed in Great Britain
by Amazon

26707740R00146